HONOR ROLL
OF
LITCHFIELD COUNTY
[CONNECTICUT]

REVOLUTIONARY SOLDIERS

Josephine Ellis Richards

HERITAGE BOOKS
2011

HERITAGE BOOKS
AN IMPRINT OF HERITAGE BOOKS, INC.

Books, CDs, and more—Worldwide

For our listing of thousands of titles see our website
at
www.HeritageBooks.com

A Facsimile Reprint
Published 2011 by
HERITAGE BOOKS, INC.
Publishing Division
100 Railroad Ave. #104
Westminster, Maryland 21157

Copyright © 1912
Mary Floyd Tallmadge Chapter
Daughters of the American Revolution
Litchfield, Connecticut

— Publisher's Notice —
In reprints such as this, it is often not possible to remove blemishes from the original. We feel the contents of this book warrant its reissue despite these blemishes and hope you will agree and read it with pleasure.

International Standard Book Numbers
Paperbound: 978-0-7884-0662-1
Clothbound: 978-0-7884-8641-8

To
JOSEPHINE ELLIS RICHARDS

whose patriotism conceived and whose faithful, patient and untiring labors of years made it possible, this Honor Roll of Litchfield County Revolutionary Soldiers is dedicated with deep affection and appreciation, by the

MARY FLOYD TALLMADGE CHAPTER
DAUGHTERS OF THE AMERICAN REVOLUTION

PREFACE

This Honor Roll of the Revolutionary Soldiers of Litchfield County, Connecticut, has been prepared by the Mary Floyd Tallmadge Chapter, Daughters of the American Revolution, with the assistance of the other Chapters of the County. It is the result of long continued and painstaking research, and while not claiming to have attained absolute completeness, it is a valuable contribution to the Revolutionary records of Connecticut.

Besides being the only compilation in one list, of names found in previous publications, it also contains many names which have never before been published.

From family records and other sources of information, some new name is still brought to light from time to time or the town from which a man served is identified.

Where the references and authorities given are not accessible to the reader, information may always be sought from the Regent of the Mary Floyd Tallmadge Chapter or the President of the Litchfield Historical Society. Many pension records are on file in the Litchfield Court House besides the store of valuable data in possession of the Chapter.

> JOSEPHINE ELLIS RICHARDS,
> CORNELIA BUXTON SMITH,
> GRACE CHAMBERLAIN PAGE,
> ADELAIDE ALMIRA BISSELL,
> EMMA LOUISE ADAMS,
> *Revolutionary Soldiers Committee.*

List of References, with Key to Abbreviations

App. for Pension,   Application for Pension.
Bark. Men,   Barkhamsted Men in the Revolution.
Biographical Review,
Blue Swamp Tax List.
Boyd's Annals.
Buell Genealogy.
Bureau of Pensions, Washington, D. C.
Chronicles of a Pioneer School,   Vanderpoel.
Conn. S. A. R. Year Book,   Connecticut Sons of American Revolution Year Book.
Cressiy's Norfolk,   History of Norfolk—Cressiy.
D. A. R. Lineage Book, also Lin. Book,   Lineage Books of N. S. D. A. R.
Gen. Jed. Huntington's Note Book,   General Jedediah Huntington's Note Book.
Gen. Reg.,   A Genealogical Register—Woodruff.
Goodwin Genealogy,
Goshen Statistics,   Goshen Statistics and Family Histories—Norton.
Grant Genealogy.
Hist. of Camden,   History of Camden, N. Y.,
Hist. of Colebrook, Ms.,   History of Colebrook—Manuscript.
Hist. of Conn.,   History of Connecticut—J. Barber.
Hist. of Cornwall,   History of Cornwall—Gold.
Hist. of Goshen,   History of Goshen—Hibbard.
Hist. of Harwinton,   History of Harwinton.
Hist. of Litchfield,   History of Litchfield—P. K. Kilbourn.
Hist. of Litchfield County,   History of Litchfield County.
Hist. of New Milford,   History of New Milford.
Hist. of Norfolk,   History of Norfolk—Cressiy.
Hist. of Sharon,   History of Sharon.
Hist. of Torrington,   History of Torrington—Orcutt.
Hist. of Waterbury,   History of Waterbury.
Hist. of Woodbury,   History of Woodbury—Cothren.
Kilbourn Gen.,   Kilbourn Genealogy—P. K. Kilbourn.
Kilbourn's Hist.,   Kilbourn's History of Litchfield.
Lists and Returns,   Revolution Lists and Returns—Connecticut Historical Society.
Litchfield & Morris Inscriptions,   Kilbourn and Payne.
Marsh Gen.,   Marsh Genealogy.
Manual of Cong. Church,   Manual of Congregational Church, Colebrook.
Notes of Ancestors,   George C. Woodruff.
Orton's Genealogy.
Patriot Daughters,   Chapter Sketches Vol. II.
Rec. Conn. Men,   Record of Connecticut Men in the Revolution.
Rev. Sol. Scrap Book,   Revolutionary Soldiers Scrap Book—Mary Floyd Tallmadge Chapter D. A. R.
Rolls and Lists,   Revolution Rolls and Lists—Connecticut Historical Society.
Stiles Ancient Windsor,   Stiles.
The Kirbys of New England.

*Lived elsewhere at time of war.
†Prison Ship Martyr.
‡Prison Ship Survivor.

Litchfield

Revolutionary Soldiers

OF

Litchfield

COMPILED BY
MARY FLOYD TALLMADGE CHAPTER
DAUGHTERS OF THE AMERICAN REVOLUTION
LITCHFIELD, CONN.

For fuller accounts of these men see original lists

Revolutionary Soldiers of Litchfield

Name	Authority	Page
Adams, Andrew, Col.,	Kilbourn's Hist.,	144
	Rec. Conn. Men,	438
Africa, Cash,	Rec. Conn. Men,	41
	Rolls and Lists,	68
	Lists and Returns,	53, 228
Agard, Hezekiah,	Rec. Conn. Men,	40
	Kilbourn's Hist.,	95
	Gen. Reg.,	7
Alcock, Giles,	Lists and Returns,	53
*Allen, Ethan, Gen.,	Kilbourn's Hist.,	93, 135
	D. A. R. Lin. Book Vol. XVIII.,	12
*Allen, Heman,	See Cornwall List, Gen Reg.,	8
Allen, John,	Rec. Conn. Men,	562
†Allen, Nathaniel,	Kilbourn's Hist.,	95, 98, 100
	Rec. Conn. Men,	40
	Gen. Reg.,	8
Aston, Elida, Serg't.,	Rec. Conn. Men,	573
Atwell, Oliver,	Rec. Conn. Men,	276
	Rev. Sol. Scrap Book,	14
Bacon, Ebenezer,	Kilbourn's Hist.,	96
	Rec. Conn. Men,	81
	Gen. Reg.,	10
Bacon, Nathaniel,	Rolls and Lists,	67
Baldwin, Abner,	Rolls and Lists,	201, 273
Baldwin, Ashbel,	Kilbourn's Hist.,	117
Baldwin, Isaac,	Dwight C. Kilbourn,	
	Gen. Reg.,	12
Baldwin, James,	Rec. Conn. Men,	41, 502, 662
	Rev. Sol. Scrap Book,	5
Baldwin, Samuel W.,	Kilbourn's Hist.,	96
	Rec. Conn. Men,	81
	Gen. Reg.,	11
Barns, Ambrose,	Rolls and Lists,	69
	Lists and Returns,	53
Barns, Amos,	Rec. Conn. Men,	276
Barns, Benjamin,	Rolls and Lists,	201
	Gen. Reg.,	14
Barns, Daniel,	Kilbourn's Hist.,	96
	Gen. Reg.,	14
Barns, Enos, Serg't.,	Rec. Conn. Men,	195
	Rolls and Lists,	69
Barns, Enos 2d,	Lists and Returns,	53
Barns, Enos 3d,	Lists and Returns,	53

Name	Authority	Page
Barns, Moses,	Rec. Conn. Men,	296
	Rolls and Lists,	201
	Gen. Reg.,	15
Barns, Orange,	App. for Pension.	
	Rec. Conn. Men,	366, 632
	Rolls and Lists,	67
	Lists and Returns,	286
Bates, Ephraim,	Rec. Conn. Men,	40
	Rolls and Lists,	103
	Lists and Returns,	53
Batterson, Stephen,	Rec. Conn. Men,	361
*Beach, Barnias,	Kilbourn's Hist.,	96, 100
	Gen. Reg.,	21
Beach, Miles, Maj.,	Kilbourn's Hist.,	125
	Rec. Conn. Men,	438
	Rev. Sol. Scrap Book,	10
Beach, Miles,	Dwight C. Kilbourn.	
†Beach, Noah,	Kilbourn's Hist.,	96, 100
	Gen. Reg.,	21
Beach, Wait,	Kilbourn's Hist.,	96
	Rec. Conn. Men,	414
Beach, Zophar,	Rolls and Lists,	201
	D. A. R. Lin. Paper, National Number, 46175.	
Beebe, Bezaleel, Col.,	Kilbourn's Hist.,	146
	Rec. Conn. Men,	40, etc.
	D A. R. Lin. Book Vol. XXI.,	305
	Lists and Returns,	88
Beecher, Burr,	D. A. R. Lin. Book Vol. XI.,	306
	Rec. Conn. Men,	408
Bend, John,	Lists and Returns,	24
Benton, Belah,	Rolls and Lists,	273
Benton, Nathaniel,	Rolls and Lists,	201
	Gen. Reg.,	27
Bill, Elijah,	Lists and Returns,	215
Bingham, Ozias,	Rec. Conn. Men,	627
(See Norfolk List).		
Birge, Benjamin,	Rolls and Lists,	201
	Gen. Reg.,	31
Birge, Beriah,	Kilbourn's Hist.,	97
	Rec. Conn. Men,	40
	Gen. Reg.,	31
Birge, James,	Kilbourn's Hist.,	97
	Rec. Conn. Men,	652, 663
	Pension Rec. for Jonathan Wright,	
	Rev. Sol. Scrap Book,	37
Bishop, Luman,	Kilbourn's Hist.,	95
	Gen. Reg.,	32, 33
Bissell, Archelaus,	App. for Pension.	
Bissell, Benjamin, Sr.,	Rec. Conn. Men,	361, 632
	Dwight C. Kilbourn.	
	Gen. Reg.,	36

LITCHFIELD

Name	Authority	Page
Bissell, Benjamin, Serg't. (which Benjamin)	App. for Pension. Rec. Conn. Men, Lists and Returns,	40, 502 54, 163
Bissell, Calvin,	Rec. Conn. Men, Rolls and Lists,	652 273
Bissell, John,	Rolls and Lists,	273
Bissell, Luther,	Woodruff's Gen. Reg.,	34
†Bissell, Zebulon,	Kilbourn's Hist., Rec. Conn. Men, D. A. R. Lineage Book, Vol. VIII.,	94, 100 423 162
Blake, Richard,	Rec. Conn. Men, Dwight C. Kilbourn. Gen. Reg.,	40 17
Blakesley, Samuel,	Rec. Conn. Men, Rolls and Lists, D. C. Kilbourn.	663 136
Bottom, John,	Rec. Conn. Men, Lists and Returns, Rev. Sol. Scrap Book,	220, 364 53, 235 12
Bradley, Aaron,	Rec. Conn. Men, Gen. Reg.,	653 19
Bradley, Abraham, Capt.,	Kilbourn's Hist., Rec. Conn. Men,	101 395
*Bradley, Daniel,	Mrs. Francis Bissell. Rolls and Lists,	48
*Bradley, Phineas, Capt.,	Rec. Conn. Men, Gen. Reg.,	546 18
Bricks, John, (Breck)	Rec. Conn. Men, Lists and Returns,	502 54
Bristol, Isaac,	Lists and Returns,	215
Brown, Joseph,	App. for Pension.	
*Buel, Asahel,	Buell Genealogy,	186
Buel, Isaac,	D. A. R. Lin. Book, Vol. XIII., Hist. of Camden, N. Y., Gen. Reg.,	307 97 41
Buel, Jonathan,	Dwight C. Kilbourn.	
(Not the Serg't. Jonathan Buel of Goshen.)		
Buel, Salmon,	Kilbourn's Hist., Rolls and Lists, Gen. Reg.,	111 265, 268 42
Buel, Solomon,	Rec. Conn. Men, Gen. Reg.,	492 41
Buell, Peter, Lieut.,	Buell Genealogy, Chapter Scrap Book, Conn. S. A. R. Year Book, 1900-3,	88 1 544
Bull, Aaron, Lieut.,	Rec. Conn. Men, Rev. Sol. Scrap Book,	271 19
Bull, Asa,	D. A. R. Lin. Book, Vol. XVIII.,	328
Bull, George,	Rolls and Lists, Gen. Reg.,	201 45

Name	Authority	Page
Burnham, Asa,	Rolls and Lists,	88
	Rev. Sol. Scrap Book,	12
	Lists and Returns,	23, 235
Burnham, Wolcott,	Bureau of Pensions by Mrs. Arnold Gregory.	
Burr, Aaron,	Kilbourn's Hist.,	92, 93
	Rev. Sol. Scrap Book,	18, 19
Byer, Return,	Rolls and Lists,	67
Canfield, Abial,	Lists and Returns,	53
*Camp, Abel,	D. A. R. Lin. Book, Vol. XX.,	258
	Gen. Reg.,	49
(Served, apparently, from Waterbury).		
Camp, Eldred,	Gen. Jed. Huntington's Note Book.	
	Lists and Returns,	53
*Camp, Ezra,	Rec. Conn. Men,	653
	Rev. Sol. Scrap Book,	24
Catlin, Abel,	Rolls and Lists,	273
Catlin, Alexander, Capt.,	Rev. Sol. Scrap Book,	12, 16
	Gen. Reg.,	52
Catlin, Ashbel,	Rolls and Lists,	273
Catlin, Bradley,	Rolls and Lists,	201
	Rec. Conn. Men,	502
	Gen. Reg.,	51
Catlin, David,	Rec. Conn. Men,	549, 653
Catlin, Eli, Capt.,	Rec. Conn. Men,	104, 194
	D. A. R. Lin. Book Vol. IX.,	196
Catlin, George,	Rec. Conn. Men,	549
	D. C. Kilbourn.	
Catlin, Isaac,	Rolls and Lists,	201
	D. C. Kilbourn.	
	Gen. Reg.,	51
Catlin, Phineas,	Rec. Conn. Men.,	481
	Gen. Reg.,	52 or 54
	D. A. R. Lineage Book Vol. XXIII.,	272
Catlin, Putnam,	Rolls and Lists,	68
	D. C. Kilbourn.	
	Lists and Returns,	53
Catlin, Samuel,	Rolls and Lists,	201
	Gen. Reg.,	51
Catlin, Theodore, Capt.,	Rec. Conn. Men,	424
	Gen. Reg.,	51
	Rev. Sol. Scrap Book,	12
Catlin, Thomas, Jr., Lieut.,	Kilbourn's Hist.,	101
	Gen. Reg.,	53
	Year Book Conn. S. A. R. 1897-9,	339
Catlin, Uriah,	Rec. Conn. Men,	562
	D. C. Kilbourn.	
Chamberlin, William,	D. A. R. Lin. Book Vol. XXVIII.,	91
Champion, Judah, Rev.,	Kilbourn's Hist.,	129
	Rec. Conn. Men,	631
Chase, Lot, Serg't.,	Rec. Conn. Men,	574

LITCHFIELD 17

Name	Authority	Page
Churchill, Oliver,	Rolls and Lists,	201
	Gen. Reg.,	65
*Clark, Abel,	Rec. Conn. Men,	541
	Rev. Sol. Scrap Book,	24
Cleaveland, Diah, (Dyer)	Rolls and Lists,	273
	Rec. Conn. Men,	197
	Gen. Jed. Huntington's Note Book.	
	Lists and Returns,	53
Clemmonds, Abijah,	Rolls and Lists,	67
Cluff, Isaac,	Rec. Conn. Men,	41, 209
(Clough)	Rolls and Lists,	111
	Lists and Returns,	53
Coe, Levi,	Rolls and Lists,	201
	Gen. Reg.,	61
Coe, Zachariah,	Lists and Returns,	215
Collens, Charles, (Collins)	Rolls and Lists,	201
	Gen. Reg.,	62
*Collins, Cyprian,	D. A. R. Lin. Book Vol. XI.,	347
	See Goshen List.	
Columbus, James,	Rolls and Lists,	68
	Lists and Returns,	53
Colyer, Joseph,	Rec. Conn. Men,	209
	Lists and Returns,	53
Cone, Abner, Lieut.,	Rolls and Lists,	201
	Rev. Sol. Scrap Book,	12
Cook, Oliver,	Hist. of Camden, N. Y.,	104, 533
Cowl, John,	Lists and Returns,	53
Cramton, Elon,	Rec. Conn. Men,	653
	Gen. Reg.,	59
	Rev. Sol. Scrap Book,	15
Crampton, James, Lieut.,	Kilbourn's Hist.,	94
(Cramton)	Gen. Reg.,	59
Crampton, Neri, Lieut.,	Rev. Sol. Scrap Book,	10
Craw, Reuben,	Rec. Conn. Men,	363
	Lists and Returns,	53
Crosby, Simon,	Rec. Conn. Men,	364
	Lists and Returns,	53
Culver, Abel,	Rolls and Lists,	69
	Rec. Conn. Men,	328, 352, 366
	Lists and Returns,	53
Culver, Ashbel, (Asabel)	Rec. Conn. Men,	41
	Gen. Reg.,	67
	D. C. Kilbourn.	
Culver, Reuben,	Rec. Conn. Men,	232
	Gen. Jed. Huntington's Note Book.	
	Gen. Reg.,	65
*Culver, Solomon,	U. S. Pension Files of 1833.	
Curtis, Zarah,	Lin. Book Vol. 26,	75
Davis, Samuel,	Rec. Conn. Men,	165, etc.
	Rolls and Lists,	55
*Dear, George 2d,	Kilbourn's Hist.,	94
	D. C. Kilbourn.	
(Blue Swamp Tax List).		

Litchfield County Revolutionary Soldiers

Name	Authority	Page
*Deming, Julius,	Rec. Conn. Men,	630
	Rev. Sol. Scrap Book,	2, 3, 17
Dennison, Chauncey,	Rec. Conn. Men,	653
	Gen. Reg.,	70
	D. C. Kilbourn.	
De Wolf, Levi,	App. for Pension.	
	Rec. Conn. Men,	633, 653
	Rev. Sol. Scrap Book,	12
Dickinson, Friend,	Kilbourn's Hist.,	96
	Rolls and Lists,	201
	D. C. Kilbourn.	
	Rec. Conn. Men,	41
Dickinson, Oliver,	Rec. Conn. Men,	663
	Rolls and Lists,	201
	Year Book Conn. S. A. R. 1897-9,	508
	Rev. Sol. Scrap Book,	37
Dixon, George,	Lists and Returns,	54
Douglas, William, Col.,	D. A. R. Lin. Book Vol. XI.,	258
Emmonds, Arrings,	Rec. Conn. Men,	569
Emons, A., (Abner or Arthur)	Rec. Conn. Men,	541
	Gen. Reg.,	73
Emons, Isaac,	Rec. Conn. Men,	502
	Gen. Reg.,	74
	D. C. Kilbourn.	
Emons, Phineas,	Rec. Conn. Men,	502
	Gen. Reg.,	74
Emons, William	Rolls and Lists,	220
	Gen. Reg.,	73
Fancher, Rufus,	Lists and Returns,	53
Farnam, John, Corp.,	Rec. Conn. Men,	364
	Rolls and Lists,	69
	Lists and Returns,	53
Farnam, Seth,	Rec. Conn. Men,	513
Fitch, Ebenezer,	D. A. R. Lin. Book Vol. XXII.,	50
Foote, Aaron, Capt.,	Rec. Conn. Men,	40
	Rolls and Lists,	224
Fox, Aaron,	Lists and Returns,	53
Frost, Joel,	Kilbourn's Hist.,	96
	Gen. Reg.,	79
Galpin, Amos,	Rec. Conn. Men,	46, 253, etc.
	Rev. Sol. Scrap Book,	5
Garnsey, Noah, (Guernsey)	Kilbourn's Hist.,	95
	Gen. Reg.,	80
	D. A. R. Lin. Book Vol. XVII.,	204
*Gatta, John I.,	Kilbourn's Hist.,	133
*Gay, Ebenezer, Lt. Col., (Served from Sharon).	D. A. R. Lin. Book Vol. XXI.,	27
*Gay, Fisher, Col.,	Kilbourn's Hist.,	106, 193
	Rec. Conn. Men,	381, 392, etc.
Gibbs, Aaron,	Rolls and Lists,	201
	Gen. Reg.,	86

LITCHFIELD 19

Name	Authority	Page
Gibbs, Benjamin, Lieut.,	Rec. Conn. Men,	79, 81
	Kilbourn's Hist.,	97
	D. A. R. Lin. Book Vol. XXVIII.,	271
Gibbs, Eliakim,	Orton Genealogy,	132
†Gibbs, Gershom,	Kilbourn's Hist.,	97, 98, 100
	Rec. Conn. Men,	422
	Gen. Reg.,	85
Gibbs, Gershom, Jr.,	App. for Pension,	
	Rec. Conn. Men,	653, 663
†Gibbs, Isaac,	Kilbourn's Hist.,	100
	Gen. Reg.,	87
Gibbs, Ithamar,	Kilbourn's Hist.,	97
	Rec. Conn. Men,	502, 549
	Gen. Reg.,	86
Gibbs, Lemuel,	Rec. Conn. Men,	81
	Gen. Reg.,	86
Gibbs, Moore, (More, Moah)	Rec. Conn. Men,	40, 276
Gibbs, Oliver,	Rolls and Lists,	201
	Gen. Reg.,	87
Gibbs, Remembrance,	Rec. Conn. Men,	81
	Gen. Reg.,	86
Gibbs, Simeon,	App. for Pension,	
	Rec. Conn. Men,	634
Gibbs, Solomon,	Rec. Conn. Men,	663
	Rev. Sol. Scrap Book,	14
Gibbs, Spencer, Serg't.,	Rec. Conn. Men,	541
	Gen. Reg.,	89
	D. C. Kilbourn.	
Gibbs, Timothy,	Rolls and Lists,	273
*Gibbs, Truman, Trumpeter,	Rec. Conn. Men,	481, 573
(See Winchester List).		
*Gibbs, Wareham, Capt.,	Rolls and Lists,	211
	Gen. Reg.,	86
	D. C. Kilbourn.	
(See Winchester List).		
Gibbs, William,	Rec. Conn. Men,	549, 663
Gibbs, William, Jr.,	Rec. Conn. Men,	481
	Gen. Reg.,	87
Gibbs, Zadok (Zadock)	Kilbourn's Hist.,	94
	Rec. Conn. Men,	549
	Gen. Reg.,	87
Gibbs, Zebulon,	Kilbourn's Hist.,	253
Gilbert, Asa,	Rec. Conn. Men,	653
	D. C. Kilbourn.	
(A pensioner of Barkhamsted).		
Gilbert, Joseph, Serg't.,	D. A. R. Lin. Book Vol. XXVIII.,	199
Guilbert, (Gilbert) Abner,	Rolls and Returns,	205
Gillett, Asa,	Rec. Conn. Men,	283
	Lists and Returns,	286
Gillett, John, Serg't.,	Rec. Conn. Men,	481
	Gen. Reg.,	92
	D. C. Kilbourn.	

Name	Authority	Page
Gillett, Othniel,	App. for Pension.	
Goff, Joseph,	Lists and Returns,	216
Goodrich, William,	Rec. Conn. Men,	298
*Goodwin, Jesse,	Goodwin Genealogy,	402, 403
	D. A. R. Lin. Book Vol. XVI.,	23
	Gen. Reg.,	97
(Served from New Hartford or Canaan).		
Goodwin, Joseph, Serg't.,	Goodwin Genealogy,	321
	Rec. Conn. Men,	549
Goodwin, Nathaniel, Capt.,	Goodwin Gen.,	273
	Kilbourn's Hist.,	107
Goodwin, Nathaniel, Jr.,	Goodwin Gen.,	302
Serg't.,	Rec. Conn. Men,	613
Goodwin, Ozias, Ensign,	Goodwin Gen.,	367
	Kilbourn's Hist.,	107, 111
	Year Book Conn. S. A. R. 1897-9,	400
†Goodwin, Phineas,	Kilbourn's Hist.,	94, 98, 100
	Rec. Conn. Men,	423
	Gen. Reg.,	97
Goodwin, Solomon,	Goodwin Gen.,	273
	Rolls and Lists,	23
Goodwin, Uri,	App. for Pension.	
Goodwin, William, Corp.,	Rec. Conn. Men,	549
	D. C. Kilbourn.	
Goslee, Solomon,	Rec. Conn. Men,	634
	Gen. Reg.,	100
	D. C. Kilbourn.	
Gould, John,	Lists and Returns,	228
Grant, Ambrose,	Grant Genealogy,	27
Grant, Elihu,	Grant Gen.,	27
	Kilbourn's Hist.,	94
Grant, Isaac,	Grant Gen.,	27
	Rolls and Lists,	69
	Lists and Returns,	53, 228
	D. A. R. Lin. Book Vol. XVII.,	38, 39
Grant, Jesse, Lieut.,	Rec. Conn. Men,	81, 104, 122
	Lists and Returns,	88
	Gen. Reg.,	84
Grant, Joel,	Grant Gen.,	27
*Grant, Roswell,	Grant Gen.,	28
(See Winchester List).		
Graves, Alexander,	Rec. Conn. Men,	569
Graves, Ezekiel,	Rec. Conn. Men,	569
Graves, Sylvanus,	Lists and Returns,	53
Green, Jacob,	Rec. Conn. Men,	583
	Rolls and Lists,	201
Griffis, James, Corp.,	Rolls and Lists,	201
	Gen. Reg.,	93
Griswold, Jacob,	Rec. Conn. Men,	562
Griswold, James,	Gen. Reg.,	93

LITCHFIELD 21

Name	Authority	Page
Griswold, John,	App. for Pension.	
	See Rev. Sol. Scrap Book,	21
Griswold, Jonathan,	Rec. Conn. Men,	81
	Gen. Reg.,	94
Griswold, Midian,	App. for Pension.	
	Rec. Conn. Men,	283
	Lists and Returns,	286
†Hall, David, Serg't.,	Kilbourn's Hist.,	96, 100
	Rec. Conn. Men,	422
	Gen. Reg.,	101
Hall, John,	Rec. Conn. Men,	40, 663
Hall, William, (3d)	Rev. Sol. Scrap Book,	25
	Gen. Reg.,	101
Hamilton, George,	Lists and Returns,	53
*Hanks, Benjamin,	D. C. Kilbourn.	
	Authority of Family.	
	Gen. Reg.,	103
Harrison, Daniel,	Rec. Conn. Men,	653
	D. C. Kilbourn.	
Harrison, David,	Rec. Conn. Men,	41
	Gen. Reg.,	104
	D. C. Kilbourn.	
Harrison, Elihu, Serg't.,	Rec. Conn. Men,	502
	Kilbourn's Hist.,	94
Harrison, Jacob,	Rec. Conn. Men,	41
	Gen. Reg.,	104, 105
	D. C. Kilbourn.	
Harrison, Lemuel,	Rec. Conn. Men,	629
	Gen. Reg.,	105
(See New Milford List).		
Harrison, Solomon,	Rec. Conn. Men,	502
	Rolls and Lists,	201, 273
Harrison, Thomas, Jr.,	Rev. Sol. Scrap Book,	15
	Gen. Reg.,	104
Hart, Tucker,	Lists and Returns,	53
Haskin (s), Abraham,	Kilbourn's Hist.,	97
	Gen. Reg.,	107
Hawley, Peter,	Lists and Returns,	54
Hays, Elijah,	Rolls and Lists,	67
Hays, Zenas,	Rolls and Lists,	67
Heath, Thomas,	Lists and Returns,	192
Henshaw, William, Jr.,	D. A. R., Lin. Book Vol. XV.,	7
	Rolls and Lists,	42, 50
Herick, Amos,	Lists and Returns,	53
Hitchcock, Abel,	Lists and Returns,	53
Hodgkis (Hotchkiss?),		
Samuel,	Lists and Returns,	203
Holcomb, Phineas,	Rolls and Lists,	67
Hopkins, Harris,	Rolls and Lists,	273
	D. A. R. Lin. Book Vol. XXVII.,	130

Litchfield County Revolutionary Soldiers

Name	Authority	Page
Horsford, Isaac,	Rolls and Lists,	201
	Gen. Reg.,	111
*Horton, Elisha,	Rec. Conn. Men,	634
	D. C. Kilbourn.	
(An officer in Mass.).		
Hotchkiss, Stephen, Serg't.,	Rec. Conn. Men,	41
	D. C. Kilbourn.	
Hotchkiss, Stephen, Serg't.,	Lists and Returns,	53
Hough, Thadeus,	Rec. Conn. Men,	362
*Hunt, Russell,	Rev. Sol. Scrap Book,	31
Jackson, Jonathan,	Rec. Conn. Men,	583
Jennings, William,	Rec. Conn. Men,	276
†Johnson, Amos, Serg't.,	Kilbourn's Hist.,	100
	Gen. Reg.,	113
	Rec. Conn. Men,	81
Johnson, Benjamin,	Rec. Conn. Men,	562
	Gen. Reg.,	115
*Johnson, Eliphalet,	Hist. of Camden, N. Y.,	305, 534
(Enlisted from Norwich).		
Johnson, John,	Lists and Returns,	53
Johnson, Rufus,	D. A. R. Lin. Book Vol. XX.,	199
Johnson, Zechariah,	Rolls and Lists,	201
	Gen. Reg.,	114
Jones, Eaton, Lieut.,	Rec. Conn. Men,	283
	Lists and Returns,	286
Jones, Harris,	App. for Pension.	
Jones, Samuel,	Rec. Conn. Men.	283
	Lists and Returns,	286
Judson, Jacob,	Rec. Conn. Men,	562
Keeney, Mark,	D. A. R. Lin. Book Vol. XVI.,	113
Kelcy, Peter,	Lists and Returns,	53
Kelley, John,	Rolls and Lists,	53
	Lists and Returns,	53, 170
Kent, Darius,	Rec. Conn. Men,	653
	Gen. Reg.,	119
	D. C. Kilbourn.	
Kilborn, Abraham,	Lists and Returns,	53
Kilborn, David,	Lists and Returns,	53
Kilbourn, Giles,	Kilbourn Gen.,	112
Kilbourn, Jehiel,	Kilbourn Gen.,	108
*Kilbourn, John, Capt.,	Kilbourn Gen.,	116
Kilbourn, Joseph,	Kilbourn Gen.,	107
Kilbourn, Roswell,	Rec. Conn. Men,	283
	Kilbourn Gen.,	108
	Lists and Returns,	286
Kilbourn, Samuel,	Kilbourn Gen.,	189
	Lists and Returns,	53
King, David, Serg't.,	Rec. Conn. Men,	41
	Gen. Reg.,	125
	D. C. Kilbourn.	

LITCHFIELD

Name	Authority	Page
Kirby, Ephraim, Lieut.,	The Kirbys of New England,	162
	Rec. Conn. Men,	273, 376
	D. A. R. Lin. Book Vol. XXVII.,	254
Knapp, Jared, Serg't.,	Rec. Conn. Men,	40, 365
	Rolls and Lists,	69
	Rev. Sol. Scrap Book,	2
	Lists and Returns,	53
*Lamson, Daniel,	Rec. Conn. Men,	653
	Rev. Sol. Scrap Book,	26
Landen, Daniel,	Rec. Conn. Men,	583
Landon, Ebenezer,	Rev. Sol. Scrap Book,	12, 13
Landon, Hazia,	Rolls and Lists,	81
Landon, James,	Rolls and Lists,	201
	Gen. Reg.,	128
Landon, Reuben,	Rolls and Lists,	201
	Gen. Reg.,	128
Landon, Seth,	Authority of Grandson.	
	Gen. Reg.,	127
Laraby, Asa,	Lists and Returns,	53
Laraby, Willet,	Lists and Returns,	54
Lerow, John, (Lerrow),	Rec. Conn. Men,	212
(Larow)	Rolls and Lists,	70
Lewis, Benjamin,	Rec. Conn. Men,	277
Lewis, Ezekiel,	Rolls and Lists,	173
	D. C. Kilbourn,	
Lewis, John, Capt.,	Rec. Conn. Men,	616
	Gen. Reg.,	132
Lewis, Joseph,	Rec. Conn. Men,	275
Lewis, Nathaniel, Serg't.,	Rec. Conn. Men,	40
	Gen. Reg.,	132
	D. C. Kilbourn,	
Lewis, William,	Rolls and Lists,	201
	Gen. Reg.,	132
Linsley, Abiel,	D. A. R. Lin. Book Vol. XVII.,	189
	Gen. Reg.,	133
Linsley, Solomon,	Rolls and Lists,	273
	Rec. Conn. Men,	541
	Lists and Returns,	286
Linsley, Timothy,	Rolls and Lists,	201, 273
	Rec. Conn. Men,	502
‡Little, James,	Kilbourn's Hist.,	97, 100
	Rec. Conn. Men,	423
	Gen. Reg.,	133
Little, Samuel, Fifer,	Rolls and Lists,	201
	Rec. Conn. Men,	583
Little, William,	Rolls and Lists,	201
	Gen. Reg.,	134
Lord, Lynde,	D. A. R. Lin. Book Vol. XVIII.,	80
†Lyman, John,	Kilbourn's Hist.,	100
	Gen. Reg.,	135
Manjent, Nicholas,	Lists and Returns,	54

Name	Authority	Page
*Mansfield, John, Capt. (From New Haven).	App. for Pension. Rev. Sol. Scrap Book,	15
Marsh, John, Capt.,	Marsh Gen., Kilbourn's Hist.,	71 107, 109
†Marsh, Timothy,	Kilbourn's Hist., Marsh Gen., Rec. Conn. Men,	97, 100 76 423
Marshall, Elisha,	Rec. Conn. Men, D. C. Kilbourn.	41
†Marshall, Oliver, (Town uncertain).	Only Ref. Kilbourn's Hist.,	97, 99, 100
Mason, Ashbel,	Rec. Conn. Men, Gen. Jed. Huntington's Note Book. Gen. Reg., Lists and Returns,	199 147 53
Mason, Elisha,	Kilbourn's Hist., Rec. Conn. Men, Rev. Sol. Scrap Book,	160 290, 663 11
Mason, John,	Rolls and Lists, Lists and Returns, Rec. Conn. Men, Rev. Sol. Scrap Book,	69 35, 53, 172 199 12
Mason, Jonathan, Lieut.,	Kilbourn's Hist., Rec. Conn. Men, D. A. R. Lin. Book Vol. IX., Gen. Reg.,	94, 109 424 196 146
Mason, Joseph,	App. for Pension, Rec. Conn. Men,	665
Mason, Luther, Corp.,	Rec. Conn. Men, D. A. R. Lin. Book Vol. IX.,	562 196
‡Mason, Thomas,	Kilbourn's Hist., Rec. Conn. Men, Gen. Reg.,	97, 100 425 147
Mazuzen, Mark,	Rolls and Lists, D. C. Kilbourn, Gen. Reg.,	9 149
McDaniel, Anthony,	Lists and Returns,	54
McIntire, Henry, (Probably a Salisbury man).	Kilbourn's Hist., Rec. Conn. Men,	97 224
McNeil, Adam,	Kilbourn's Hist.,	97
McNiel, Archibald, Jr.,	Rec. Conn. Men, Rolls and Lists, Gen. Reg.,	548 209 136
†McNiel, Alexander 3d,	Kilbourn's Hist., Gen. Reg.,	97, 100 137
Meleck, Ebed,	Lists and Returns,	54
Merrill, Nathaniel (Nathan)	App. for Pension. Rec. Conn. Men,	630
Mix, Eli,	Lists and Returns,	53

LITCHFIELD

Name	Authority	Page
Morris, James, Capt.,	Kilbourn's Hist.,	101, 128
	Rec. Conn. Men,	194
Morris, Richard,	Kilbourn's Hist.,	132
Moss, Levi, (Levy)	Rec. Conn. Men,	663
	Gen. Reg.,	152
	Rev. Sol. Scrap Book,	20
Moss, Linos,	Rec. Conn. Men,	502
	D. C. Kilbourn.	
Moulthrop, Moses,	Rec. Conn. Men,	364
Munger, Daniel,	Rolls and Lists,	90
	Rec. Conn. Men,	365
	Rev. Sol. Scrap Book,	12
	Lists and Returns,	35, 54, 235, 355
Negro, George,	Lists and Returns,	286
Negro, Jack,	Lists and Returns,	54
Norton, John,	Rec. Conn. Men,	583
*Odell, William,	D. A. R. Lin. Book Vol. XIII.,	336
	Rec. Conn. Men,	653
(Served from Redding).		
Olcott, Giles,	Rolls and Lists,	68
	Rec. Conn. Men,	328, 368
†Olmstead, David, Capt.,	Kilbourn's Hist.,	100
	Rec. Conn. Men,	616
	Gen. Reg.,	158
Orton, Azariah,	Orton Genealogy,	136
	Gen. Reg.,	161
	D. A. R. Lin. Book Vol. XXVII.,	12
Orton, Darius,	Orton Gen.,	136
	Rec. Conn. Men,	502, 541
	Gen. Reg.,	160
	Lists and Returns,	203
Orton, Eliada,	Orton Gen.,	134
	Rec. Conn. Men,	639
Orton, Gideon,	Orton Gen.,	130
	Rec. Conn. Men,	502
Orton, Lemuel,	Orton Gen.,	139
	Rec. Conn. Men,	276
	D. A. R. Lin. Book Vol. XIV.,	328
Orton, Samuel,	Orton Gen.,	130
	Rec. Conn. Men,	502
Osborn, Ethan,	Kilbourn's Hist.,	97
	Patriots' Daughters,	342
	D. A. R. Lin. Book Vol. XXVII.,	89
Osborn, Isaac,	Rolls and Lists,	201
	Gen. Reg.,	162
Osborn, Jeremiah,	Rolls and Lists,	201
	Rec. Conn. Men,	228
	Gen. Reg.,	162
Osborn, John, Capt.,	Rolls and Lists,	201, 224
	Rec. Conn. Men,	653
	D. C. Kilbourn.	
	Gen. Reg.,	163

Name	Authority	Page
Osborne, Eliada, Capt.,	Rec. Conn. Men,	663
	Rev. Sol. Scrap Book,	7
Owen, Thomas,	Lists and Returns,	54
Page, Abel,	Rec. Conn. Men,	298
Page, Asa,	Rolls and Lists,	201
Page, Daniel,	Rolls and Lists,	201
Palmer, Benjamin,	Rec. Conn. Men,	40
	Rolls and Lists,	273
	Rev. Sol. Scrap Book,	12
	Lists and Returns,	37, 54, 173, 356
Palmer, Chileon,	App. for Pension.	
	Rec. Conn. Men,	276
Parmeley, Amos, Lieut.,	Rolls and Lists,	201
	Gen. Reg.,	168
	Rev. Sol. Scrap Book,	12
Parmeley, Joel, (Parmelee)	Rec. Conn. Men,	277, 502
	Gen. Reg.,	168
†Parmeley, John,	Kilbourn's Hist.,	97, 100
(Parmelee)	Rec. Conn. Men,	423
	Gen. Reg.,	168
†Parmeley, Solomon,	Kilbourn's Hist.,	97, 100
(Parmelee)	Rec. Conn. Men,	423
	Gen. Reg.,	168
Parker, Isaac,	Lists and Returns,	54
Parker, Joseph, Dr.,	D. A. R. Lin. Book Vol. VI.,	31
	Gen. Reg.,	167
Parsons, Eliphaz,	Kilbourn's Hist.,	97
	Gen. Reg.,	170
Peck, Asahel,	Rec. Conn. Men,	180
	Rev. Sol. Scrap Book,	11
Peck Elijah,	Rec. Conn. Men,	81, 502
	Gen. Reg.,	172
Peck, John, Jr.,	Rec. Conn. Men,	482
Peck, Levi,	Rec. Conn. Men,	40
	Kilbourn's Hist.,	111
Peck, Moses,	Rolls and Lists,	201
	Rec. Conn. Men,	569
	Gen. Reg.,	173
	D. C. Kilbourn.	
Peck, Paul,	Kilbourn's Hist.,	111
Peck, Philo,	Rev. Sol. Scrap Book,	5
Peck, Reeve,	Rec. Conn. Men,	481
	D. A. R. Lin. Paper, Nat. No. 48,	326
Phelps, Edward 3d,	Gen. Reg.,	178
Phelps, John,	Rec. Conn. Men,	549
	Gen. Reg.,	178
	D. C. Kilbourn.	
Phillips, Gideon,	Rolls and Lists,	80, 273
	Rec. Conn. Men,	653

LITCHFIELD

Name	Authority	Page
Pierce, John,	Rec. Conn. Men,	313
	Chronicles of a Pioneer School,	339, 353
Pilgrim, Thomas,	Rec. Conn. Men,	177, 636
Plant, Stephen,	Rolls and Lists,	201
	Gen. Reg.,	171
Plant, Timothy,	Rec. Conn. Men,	200
	Gen. Reg.,	170
	Rev. Sol. Scrap Book,	12
	Lists and Returns,	37, 54
Plumb (e), Ebenezer,	Rec. Conn. Men,	481
	Gen. Reg.,	180
Plumb, Henry,	Kilbourn's Hist.,	97
	Gen. Reg.,	181
Pond, Beriah,	App. for Pension.	
	Rec. Conn. Men,	636
	Gen. Reg.,	179
Post, Ward, Corp.,	Rec. Conn. Men,	583
Potter, Joel,	App. for Pension.	
Price, Paul,	App. for Pension.	
	Rec. Conn. Men,	363
	Lists and Returns,	54
(A resident of Goshen but enlisted in Litchfield).		
*Ranney, Stephen, Maj.,	Rev. Sol. Scrap Book,	3
(Of Bethlehem. See Woodbury List).		
Ray, William, (Rea)	Gen. Reg.,	182
Reeve, Tapping,	Kilbourn's Hist.,	156
Rich, Amos,	Rec. Conn. Men,	282
Rich, Caesar,	Gen. Jed. Huntington's Note Book.	
	Rec. Conn. Men,	214
Riggs, Jeremiah, Corp.,	Rolls and Lists,	201
	Gen. Reg.,	183
Roberts, Thomas,	Lists and Returns,	54
Robins, John,	Rec. Conn. Men,	569
	Blue Swamp Tax List.	
Rogers, Joseph,	Lists and Returns,	199
Ross, Simeon,	Rolls and Lists,	273
	Lists and Returns,	54
Rosseter, Samuel,	Rec. Conn. Men,	81
	Rolls and Lists,	111
	Lists and Returns,	38, 54, 173
Russell, John,	Rolls and Lists,	201
	Gen. Reg.,	186
Royal, John,	Lists and Returns,	54
Sacket, Buel,	Lists and Returns,	205
Sales, William,	Lists and Returns,	54
Sanford, Jonah,	Rec. Conn. Men,	500
Sanford, Joseph,	Kilbourn's Hist.,	94
	Rolls and Lists,	201
	Rec. Conn. Men,	549
	Rev. Sol. Scrap Book,	37
Sanford, Moses,	Rec. Conn. Men,	502, 541, 583

Name	Authority	Page
Sanford, Oliver,	Rec. Conn. Men, Gen. Reg., D. C. Kilbourn.	493 188
Sanford, Solomon,	Rec. Conn. Men,	562
Sanford, Zaccheus,	Rec. Conn. Men,	294
Seelye, Benjamin,	Rec. Conn. Men, Blue Swamp Tax List. D. C. Kilbourn.	116
Seelye, David,	Rec. Conn. Men, Rev. Sol. Scrap Book, Lists and Returns,	225 12 54
Seelye, Ebenezer,	Rec. Conn. Men, Lists and Returns,	283, 502 286
Seelye, John,	App. for Pension. Lists and Returns,	54, 235
Seelye, Seth,	Rec. Conn. Men,	298
Seelye, Zadok,	Rec. Conn. Men,	569
Seymour, Moses, Maj.,	Kilbourn's Hist., D. A. R. Lin. Book Vol. IV.,	128, 157 75
Seymour, Samuel, Capt.,	Rec. Conn. Men, Gen. Reg., D. A. R. Lin. Book Vol. XXIII.,	653 193 295
*Sheldon, Elisha, Col., (Enlisted from Salisbury).	Kilbourn's Hist.,	128
Sheldon, Thomas,	Rec. Conn. Men,	562
Shelley, John, (Alias Kelly)	Rolls and Lists, Rev. Sol. Scrap Book, Lists and Returns,	90 12 40, 235
Shethar, John, Capt.,	Rec. Conn. Men, Lists and Returns,	272, 481 53
Simpson, John,	Lists and Returns,	54
Smith, David, Gen.,	Kilbourn's Hist.,	128
*Smith, Eli, Ensign,	Rec. Conn. Men, Biographical Review, Rev. Sol. Scrap Book,	616 433 15
Smith, Elisha,	Rec. Conn. Men,	63, 277
Smith, Henry,	Rolls and Lists, Rev. Sol. Scrap Book, Lists and Returns,	68 12 39, 54, 175
Smith, Jacob, Serg't.,	Rec. Conn. Men, Gen. Reg., D. C. Kilbourn.	502 203
Smith, John,	Rec. Conn. Men, Kilbourn's Hist., Lists and Returns,	226 96 54
Smith, Jonathan, (Jr.)	Rec. Conn. Men, Gen. Reg., D. C. Kilbourn. Lists and Returns,	41 204 54, 235
Smith, Joshua, Jr.,	Kilbourn's Hist., Gen. Reg.,	95 203

LITCHFIELD 29

Name	Authority	Page
Smith, Moses,	Rec. Conn. Men,	583
Smith, Nathaniel,	App. for Pension.	
Smith, Reuben, Dr.,	Kilbourn's Hist.,	108
	Lists and Returns,	54, 286
Smith, Stephen,	Rec. Conn. Men,	63
	Rolls and Lists,	273
Spencer, Ephraim,	Rec. Conn. Men,	637
	Gen. Reg.,	199
Sperry, Enoch,	Rolls and Lists,	273
	Rec. Conn. Men,	328, 352
	Lists and Returns,	54
Stanard, Samuel,	Rolls and Lists,	69, 139
	Lists and Returns,	39, 54, 175
Stanley, Earl,	Rec. Conn. Men,	549
	D. C. Kilbourn.	
†Stanley, Timothy,	Kilbourn's Hist.,	97, 100
	Rec. Conn. Men,	422
	Gen. Reg.,	190 or 191
Stanton, William, Capt.,	Kilbourn's Hist.,	128, 262
	Rec. Conn. Men,	110, 271
Stevenson, Adam,	Lists and Returns,	54
Stewart, Daniel,	D. A. R. Lin. Book Vol. XXII.,	337
Stocker, Thadeus,	Rec. Conn. Men,	40, 653
	D. C. Kilbourn.	
†Stoddard, Aaron,	Kilbourn's Hist.,	97, 100
	Rec. Conn. Men,	423
	Gen. Reg.,	209
	D. A. R. Lin. Book Vol. XXVIII.,	60
Stoddard, Bryant, Capt.,	Kilbourn's Hist.,	94
	Rolls and Lists,	212
	Rev. Sol. Scrap Book,	27
Stoddard, David, Lieut.,	Rolls and Lists,	201
	Gen. Reg.,	208
Stoddard, Daniel,	Rolls and Lists,	82
	Rev. Sol. Scrap Book,	10
Stoddard, Jesse,	Rolls and Lists,	201
	Rev. Sol. Scrap Book,	39
Stoddard, Obed,	Kilbourn's Hist.,	94
	Gen. Reg.,	210
Stone, Benjamin,	Rolls and Lists,	273
	Rev. Sol. Scrap Book,	6
Stone, Ira,	Kilbourn's Hist.,	97
	Gen. Reg.,	213
Stone, Jonah,	Gen. Reg.,	212
	Mrs. Francis Bissell.	
Stone, Josiah,	Rolls and Lists,	90
(Alias Joseph)	Rev. Sol. Scrap Book,	12
	Lists and Returns,	40, 54, 235
Stone, Levi,	Lin. Book Vol. XXIII.,	299
Stone, Seth,	Rec. Conn. Men,	279
Stone, Sylvanus,	Rec. Conn. Men,	402
(Sylvenus)	Gen. Reg.,	212

Litchfield County Revolutionary Soldiers

Name	Authority	Page
‡Stone, Thomas,	Rev. Sol. Scrap Book,	13
	Rec. Conn. Men,	663
Strickland, David,	Lists and Returns,	54
Strong, Jedediah,	Kilbourn's Hist.,	106
†Stuart, Jared, (Steward)	Kilbourn's Hist.,	100
	Rec. Conn. Men,	423
	Gen. Reg.,	200
Sweet, John,	Rec. Conn. Men,	81
	Gen. Huntington's Note Book.	
	Lists and Returns,	54
*Tallmadge, Benjamin, Maj.,	Kilbourn's Hist.,	150
	D. A. R. Lin. Book Vol. III.,	232
Taylor, Benjamin,	Kilbourn's Hist.,	94
	Rec. Conn. Men,	226
	Lists and Returns,	54
Taylor, Ebenezer,	Rec. Conn. Men,	40
	D. A. R. Lin. Book Vol. XIV.,	338
Taylor, Elisha,	Rec. Conn. Men,	46, 541, 663
	Rev. Sol. Scrap Book,	37
†Taylor, Joel,	Rolls and Lists,	273
	Rec. Conn. Men,	423
	Kilbourn's Hist.,	100
Taylor, John,	Rec. Conn. Men,	325
	Year Book Conn. S. A. R. 1897-9,	293
	D. A. R. Lin. Book Vol. XXV.,	89
Taylor, Moses,	Kilbourn's Hist.,	94
	Gen. Reg.,	220
Taylor, Simeon,	App. for Pension.	
(Went as substitute for New Milford man).		
Taylor, Zebulon 2d, Capt.,	Rec. Conn. Men,	548
	Rev. Sol. Scrap Book,	12, 16
	Gen. Reg.,	221
Thomas, Joseph,	Rec. Conn. Men,	502
	Gen. Reg.,	222
	D. C. Kilbourn.	
Throop, Benjamin,	Rolls and Lists,	201
	Gen. Reg.,	223
Todd, Samuel,	D. A. R. Lin. Book Vol. XVI.,	27
	Lists and Returns,	54
Tracy, Uriah,	Rec. Conn. Men,	28
Tracy, Silas,	Rec. Conn. Men,	252
Trowbridge, Isaac,	Lists and Retunrs,	54
Trumbull, Ezekiel,	App. for Pension.	
	Rec. Conn. Men,	41
Tuttle, Levi,	Gen. Reg.,	225
	Rev. Sol. Scrap Book,	12
	Lists and Returns,	42, 54, 235
Underwood, James,	D. A. R. Lin. Book Vol. III.,	147
†Vaill, Samuel,	Kilbourn's Hist.,	97, 100
	Rec. Conn. Men,	422
	Gen. Reg.,	226
Vaughn, John,	Lists and Returns,	54

LITCHFIELD 31

Name	Authority	Page
Vaughn, Samuel,	Lists and Returns,	54
Wadsworth, Elijah, Gen.,	Kilbourn's Hist.,	128, 264
	Rec. Conn. Men,	271
Wadsworth, Epaphras,	Kilbourn's Hist.,	96
	Rec. Conn. Men,	81
	Gen. Reg.,	227
*Wallace, Nathaniel L.,	Rec. Conn. Men,	481
	Gen. Reg.,	227
Wallace, Richard, Corp.,	Rec. Conn. Men,	549
	D. C. Kilbourn.	
	Gen. Reg.,	228
Warren, Abijah, (Ahijah)	Rolls and Lists,	201
	Gen. Reg.,	229
Waugh, Alexander, Capt.,	Kilbourn's Hist.,	107
	Rolls and Lists,	201
	Gen. Reg.,	230
	Hist. of Camden, N. Y.,	502
Waugh, Joseph,	Rec. Conn. Men,	583
Waugh, Samuel, Capt.,	App. for Pension.	
	Rec. Conn. Men,	637
	Rev. Sol. Scrap Book,	28
	Lists and Returns,	54
Waugh, Thadeus, Dr.,	Rolls and Lists,	69
	Rec. Conn. Men,	649
	D. A. R. Lin. Book Vol. VIII.,	142
	Rev. Sol. Scrap Book,	28
	Lists and Returns,	54
Way, Asa,	Rec. Conn. Men,	291
Way, Ira,	Rec. Conn. Men,	239, 569
	D. C. Kilbourn.	
	An Ara Way in Gen. Reg.,	231
Way, John,	Rolls and Lists,	273
	Rec. Conn. Men,	81
Way, Selah, (Seeley)	Rolls and Lists,	201
	Rec. Conn. Men,	562
Webster, Benjamin, Jr.,	Rolls and Lists,	201
	Year Book Conn. S. A. R. 1900-3,	637
	Gen. Reg.,	231
	D. C. Kilbourn.	
Webster, Charles,	Rec. Conn. Men,	181
	Gen. Reg.,	231
	D C. Kilbourn.	
Webster, Elijah,	Rolls and Lists,	201
	Rec. Conn. Men,	502
	Gen. Reg.,	231
Webster, Justus,	Gen. Reg.,	232
Webster, Michael,	Rec. Conn. Men,	562
Webster, Obed,	Rec. Conn. Men,	562
Webster, Reuben,	Rolls and Lists,	201
	Gen. Reg.,	237
Webster, Stephen, Corp.,	Rec. Conn. Men,	497
	Gen. Reg.,	232
	D. C. Kilbourn.	

Name	Authority	Page
Webster, Timothy, Jr.,	Rec. Conn. Men,	179
	Gen. Reg.,	233
	D. C. Kilbourn.	
*Weed, Ezra,	Rec. Conn. Men,	637
	Rev. Sol. Scrap Book,	7
Welch, David, Maj.,	Kilbourn's Hist.,	106
	Rec. Conn. Men,	39
	D. A. R. Lin. Book Vol. VIII.,	16
	Gen. Reg.,	235
Welch, John, Lieut.,	Rec. Conn. Men,	282, 283
	D. A. R. Lin Book Vol. VIII.,	16
Welch, John 2d,	Lists and Returns,	286
Wetmore, David,	Rolls and Lists,	201
	Gen. Reg.,	237
Whittlesey, Roger N.,	Kilbourn's Hist.,	94
	Gen. Reg.,	238
	Rev. Sol. Scrap Book,	29
Wickwire, Grant,	Rec. Conn. Men,	663
	Rev. Sol. Scrap Book,	28
Wilcox, Philemon,	Rolls and Lists,	273
	Lists and Returns,	54
Wolcott, Oliver, Gen.,	Kilbourn's Hist.,	107
	Rec. Conn. Men,	429
Wolcott, Oliver, Jr.,	Kilbourn's Hist.,	110
Woodcock, Samuel, Serg't.,	Rolls and Lists,	69, 271
	Rec. Conn. Men,	156
	Lists and Returns,	54
Woodruff, Andrew,	Rolls and Lists,	201
	Gen. Reg.,	261
Woodruff, Baldwin,	Rec. Conn. Men,	276
Woodruff, Benjamin, (Jr.)	Rec. Conn. Men,	271
	Gen. Reg.,	256
Woodruff, Charles, Jr.,	Kilbourn's Hist.,	94
	Gen. Reg.,	256
Woodruff, Jacob,	Notes on Ancestors by Geo. C. Woodruff.	
Woodruff, James,	Kilbourn's Hist.,	94
	Rev. Sol. Scrap Book,	4
Woodruff, John,	Rolls and Lists,	273
	Rec. Conn. Men,	502
Woodruff, Jonah, Serg't.,	Rec. Conn. Men,	40
	Gen. Reg.,	257
	D. C. Kilbourn.	
‡Woodruff, Oliver,	Kilbourn's Hist.,	94, 101
	Rec. Conn. Men,	422
	Gen. Reg.,	257
Woodruff, Philo,	Rolls and Lists,	273
	Rec. Conn. Men,	513
Woodruff, Samuel,	Rec. Conn. Men,	40
	Gen. Reg.,	258
Woodruff, Solomon,	Rolls and Lists,	201, 273
	Rec. Conn. Men,	502

Name	Authority	Page
Wooster, Ephraim,	Rec. Conn. Men,	481, 549
	D. C. Kilbourn.	
	Gen. Reg.,	264
Wooster, Lemuel,	Rec. Conn. Men,	549
	Gen. Reg.,	264
	D. C. Kilbourn.	
Wright, James,	Rec. Conn. Men,	81
	Rolls and Lists,	68
	Lists and Returns,	42, 54, 177
Wright, Jonathan, Ensign,	Rec. Conn. Men,	541
	Rev. Sol. Scrap Book,	37

Barkhamsted

Revolutionary Soldiers

OF

Barkhamsted

PRESENTED, AND IN PART COMPILED, BY
GREEN WOODS CHAPTER
DAUGHTERS OF THE AMERICAN REVOLUTION
WINSTED, CONN.

For fuller accounts of these men see original lists

Revolutionary Soldiers of Barkhamsted

Name	Authority	Page
Adams, Richard,	Barkhamsted Men,	11
	Rec. Conn. Men,	49
Allen, David,	Bark. Men,	11
	Rec. Conn. Men,	165
*Allen, Joel,	Bark. Men,	11
	Rec. Conn. Men,	382, 396
(Served from Farmington).		
(Two if not three of this name in the service).		
Allen, Jonathan,	Bark. Men,	40
	Rec. Conn. Men,	10, 165
Allyn, Aaron,	Bark. Men,	11
	Rec. Conn. Men,	382
Allyn, Pelatiah, Jr.,	Rec. Conn. Men,	495
	Bark. Men,	12
Andrews, Benjamin,	Bark. Men,	40
	Rec. Conn. Men,	663
Andruss, Nehemiah,	Bark. Men,	12
	Rec. Conn. Men,	472
Austin, James,	Bark. Men,	12
	Rec. Conn. Men,	17, 540
Austin, John,	Bark. Men,	12
	Rec. Conn. Men,	148, 203, 471
Balcom, Elias,	Bark. Men,	12
	Rec. Conn. Men,	196, 327, 641
Barber, Abraham,	Bark. Men,	13
	Rec. Conn. Men,	21, 495, 540, 640
Barber, David,	Bark. Men,	13
	Rec. Conn. Men,	623
Barber, Ephraim,	Bark. Men,	13
	Rec. Conn. Men,	472
Barber, Jacob,	Bark. Men,	13
	Rec. Conn. Men,	21, 473
Barber, Reuben,	Bark. Men,	13
	Rec. Conn. Men,	21, 203
Benham, Elias,	Bark. Men,	13
	Rec. Conn. Men,	17
Bennett, Daniel,	Bark. Men,	40
(Four or five Daniel Bennetts in the Army).		
*Bishop, Seth,	Bark. Men,	14
	Rec. Conn. Men,	547, 652, 663
Blakesley, Obed,	Bark. Men,	14
	Conn. Pension List,	641

Litchfield County Revolutionary Soldiers

Name	Authority	Page
*Breeton, William,	Bark. Men,	41
	Rec. Conn. Men,	511
(Probably served from Canton).		
*Brownson, Josiah,	Bark. Men,	41
	Rec. Conn. Men,	417
(Perhaps from Canton).		
*Brister, David,	Bark. Men,	41
	Rec. Conn. Men,	480
Bumpus, Simeon,	Bark. Men,	41
	Rec. Conn. Men,	506
*Burwell, Daniel,	Bark. Men,	14
	Rec. Conn. Men,	652
(Served from Milford).		
Case, Abner,	Bark. Men,	14
	Rec. Conn. Men,	473
Case, Amos,	Bark. Men,	14
Case, Elijah,	Bark. Men,	15
	Rec. Conn. Men,	17, 196
Case, Elijah, Jr.,	Bark. Men,	15
	Rec. Conn. Men,	87
Case, Ezra,	Bark. Men,	15
	Rec. Conn. Men,	562
*Case, Giles,	Bark. Men,	41
	Rec. Conn. Men,	499, 536
*Case, Humphrey,	Bark. Men,	15
(Served perhaps from Bloomfield).		
Case, Oliver,	Bark. Men,	15
	Rec. Conn. Men,	382, 623
	Pension List,	651
Case, Ozias,	Bark. Men,	41
	Rec. Conn. Men,	470
Case, Richard,	Bark. Men,	41
	Rec. Conn. Men,	473
Case, William,	Bark. Men,	16
	Rec. Conn. Men,	17, 50
Catlin, Abraham,	Bark. Men,	16
	Rec. Conn. Men,	40
Chubb, Alexander,	Bark. Men,	16
	Rec. Conn. Men,	540
*Clark, Uzziel,	Bark. Men,	16
	Rec. Conn. Men,	540
(From Colchester or East Haddam).		
*Cleveland, Rufus, Corp.,	Bark. Men,	17
	Rec. Conn. Men,	87
(From East Windsor or Ellington).		
Collins, Nathaniel,	Bark. Men,	17
	Rec. Conn. Men,	17, 471, 291
	Pension List,	651
(Two Nathaniel Collins in the service).		
*Cossett, Timothy,	Bark. Men,	17
	Rec. Conn. Men,	87, 472, 495
(Probably served from Granby).		

BARKHAMSTED 41

Name	Authority	Page
Crane, Ebenezer,	Bark. Men,	17
	Rec. Conn. Men,	17, 551
(Two Ebenezer Cranes in the service).		
Crane, Jeremiah,	Bark. Men,	18
	Rec. Conn. Men,	471
Crane, John, Jr.,	Bark. Men,	18
	Rec. Conn. Men,	51
	Pension List,	642
(Two John Cranes in the service).		
Darby, John,	Bark. Men,	18
	Rec. Conn. Men,	63
Elwell, Joshua,	Bark. Men,	18
	Rec. Conn. Men,	17, 471
Eno, Samuel,	Rolls and Returns,	145
Foot, John,	Bark. Men,	42
	Rec. Conn. Men,	21, 499
*Ford, Cephas,	Bark. Men,	18
(From near Plymouth).		
Foster, David,	Bark. Men,	42
	Rec. Conn. Men,	642
Fox, Ebenezer,	Bark. Men,	42
	Rec. Conn. Men,	290, 639
Frazier, John,	Bark. Men,	18
	Rec. Conn. Men,	513
*Fuller, Abijah,	Bark. Men,	19
	Rec. Conn. Men,	582
	Pension List,	634
(Credited to Chatham).		
Gaines, Moses,	Bark. Men,	19
	Rec. Conn. Men,	473
(Served from Simsbury).		
*Giddings, Thomas,	Bark. Men,	42
	Rec. Conn. Men,	472
*Gilbert, Asa,	Bark. Men,	19
	Rec. Conn. Men,	17, 473
(Served probably from New Hartford).		
(Two Asa Gilberts in the service).		
Gilbert, Theodore,	D. A. R. Lineage Book Vol. XXIII.,	186
	Bark. Men,	19
(Two Theodore Gilberts in the service).		
Goss, Thomas,	Bark. Men,	19
	Rec. Conn. Men,	17, 471
*Griffin, Ezra,	Bark. Men,	20
	Rec. Conn. Men,	583
(Served from Simsbury).		
Harris, William,	Bark. Men,	42
	Rec. Conn. Men,	639
*Hart, Hawkins,	Bark. Men,	20
	Rec. Conn. Men,	406
(Served from Wallingford). (Meriden).		
*Hart, Hawkins,	Bark. Men,	20
	Rec. Conn. Men,	480, 444
(Served from Southington).		

Name	Authority	Page
Hatch, Nathan,	Bark. Men,	20
	Rec. Conn. Men,	562
(Two Nathan Hatches in service).		
*Hayden, Samuel,	Bark. Men,	21
	Rec. Conn. Men,	459
(Served from Goshen).		
Hayes, Dudley,	Bark. Men,	21
	Rec. Conn. Men,	647
Hayes, Seth,	Bark. Men,	21
	Rec. Conn. Men,	536
Hayes, Zenas,	Bark. Men,	21
	Rec. Conn. Men,	174
Hitchcock, Oliver,	Bark. Men,	21
Holcomb, James,	Bark. Men,	42
	Rec. Conn. Men,	117
*Holcomb, Phineas,	Bark. Men,	42
	Rec. Conn. Men,	570, 652
*Hoskins, David, Jr.,	Bark. Men,	22
	Rec. Conn. Men,	536
(Of Simsbury).		
*Hough, Caleb,	Bark. Men,	22
	Rec. Conn. Men,	42
Hudson, John,	Bark. Men,	22
	Rec. Conn. Men,	151, 471
Humphrey, Ambrose,	Bark. Men,	22
	Rec. Conn. Men,	471, 540
*Humphrey, Solomon,	Bark. Men,	22
	Rec. Conn. Men,	49, 474, 652
(Served from what is now Canton).		
*Hungerford, James,	Bark Men,	23
	Rec. Conn. Men,	63, 570
(Credited to Hartland).		
Ives, John,	Bark. Men,	23
	Rec. Conn. Men,	17, 199, 299, 329
*Ives, Nathaniel,	Bark. Men,	23
	Rec. Conn. Men,	470
(Supposed to have served from New Hartford).		
*Johnson, Jonathan,	Bark. Men,	23
	Rec. Conn. Men,	399
(Of Enfield, or near there. Two Jonathan Johnsons in service).		
*Jones, Asa,	Bark. Men,	42
	Rec. Conn. Men,	646
(From Branford).		
Jones, Benjamin,	Bark. Men,	24
Jones, Benoni,	Rec. Conn. Men,	471
Jones, Israel, Jr.,	Bark. Men,	24
	Rec. Conn. Men,	61, 218, 624
*Jones, Richard,	Bark. Men,	43
	Rec. Conn. Men,	506
(Served from Colchester).		

BARKHAMSTED 43

Name	Authority	Page
Jones, Samuel,	Bark. Men,	25
	Rec. Conn. Men,	471
(Five Samuel Jones in the service).		
Jones, Thomas,	Bark. Men,	25
	Rec. Conn. Men,	472
(Five Thos. Jones in the service).		
King, Jonathan,	Bark. Men,	25
	Rec. Conn. Men,	17, 540
(Three Jonathan Kings in the service).		
Langdon, John,	Bark. Men,	25
	Rec. Conn. Men,	513
Lawrence, Bigelow,	Bark. Men,	25
	Rec. Conn Men,	472
Leavit, Jonathan,	Bark. Men,	43
	Rec. Conn. Men,	513
*Lee, David,	Bark. Men,	26
	Rec. Conn. Men,	166, 653, 663
(Born Farmington. Came from Granby about 1800.)		
(Another Conn. David Lee a pensioner in Vermont.)		
*Lee, Thomas,	Bark. Men,	43
	Rec. Conn. Men,	49, 396, 620
(A soldier from Farmington. Lived also in New Hartford.)		
Lewis, Joshua,	Bark. Men,	26
Lewis, Nathaniel,	Bark. Men,	26
	Rec. Conn. Men,	471, 540
(Two Nathaniel Lewis in the service).		
Little, William,	Bark. Men,	26
	Rec. Conn. Men,	536
(Two, if not three William Littles in the service.)		
*Loomis, Elijah,	Bark. Men,	43
	Rec. Conn. Men,	88
(A soldier from Bolton.)		
*Loomis, Roger,	Bark. Men,	43
	Rec. Conn. Men,	254
(A soldier from Bolton.)		
Mallory, Amasa,	Bark. Men,	26
*Marsh, John, (not Mash	Bark. Men,	27
as in Rec. Conn. Men)	Rec. Conn. Men,	345
(Served from New Hartford.)		
(Two John Marshes in the service.)		
*Mentor, Daniel,	Bark. Men,	27
	Rec. Conn. Men,	50
(Was of Colchester.)		
Merrill, John, 4th,	Bark. Men,	27
Merritt, Peter,	Bark. Men,	27
	Rec. Conn. Men,	21
(Two Peter Merritts in the service.)		
*Messenger, Abner,	Bark. Men,	27
	Rec. Conn. Men,	570
(Credited to Simsbury.)		
Messenger, Elijah,	Bark. Men,	28
	Rec. Conn. Men,	108, 540, 562

LITCHFIELD COUNTY REVOLUTIONARY SOLDIERS

Name	Authority	Page
*Mills, Gideon,	Bark. Men,	28
	Rec. Conn. Men,	17, 49, 616
(Was of Simsbury, now Canton.)		
McNeil, James,	Bark. Men,	28
	Rec. Conn. Men,	570
Monson, Wait,	Bark. Men,	30
Moor, Saunders,	Bark. Men,	43
	Rec. Conn. Men,	21, 473
*Moore, William,	Bark. Men,	28
(Was of Windsor.)		
(Two, if not three William Moores in service.)		
Morrison, William,	Bark. Men,	43
	Rec. Conn. Men,	643
Moses, Ashbill, [Ashbell]	Bark. Men,	29
	Rec. Conn. Men,	495
	Pension List,	653
	D. A. R. Lineage Book, Vol. XXIV.,	172
Moses, Martin,	Bark. Men,	29
	Rec. Conn. Men,	224, 652
	Pension List,	653
*Moses, Seba,	Bark. Men,	29
	Rec. Conn. Men,	495, 536
(Served from Simsbury.)		
Mott, Samuel,	Lists and Returns,	189
Munson, Ephraim,	Bark. Men,	29
	Rec. Conn. Men,	116
Munson, Medad,	Bark. Men,	29, 30
Neal, William,	Bark. Men,	44
	Rec. Conn. Men,	536
Newell, Riverius,	Bark. Men,	30
	Rec. Conn. Men,	247
Newell, Solomon,	Bark. Men,	30
	Rec. Conn. Men,	562
(Served from Southington.)		
Norton, John,	Bark. Men,	30
	Rec. Conn. Men,	17, 471
(Three John Nortons in the service).		
Palmer, Benjamin,	Bark. Men,	44
	Rec. Conn. Men,	200
(At least three of this name in the service).		
*Parker, Benjamin,	Bark. Men,	30
	Rec. Conn. Men,	42, 643
(Served from Hartland. Three, possibly four of this name in service).		
Parker, Benjamin, Jr.,	Bark. Men,	31
	Rec. Conn. Men,	472
*Perkins, Gideon,	Bark. Men,	44
	Rec. Conn. Men,	385
(Of Suffield).		
Phelps, Abijah,	Bark. Men,	31
	Rec. Conn. Men,	166, 631

BARKHAMSTED

Name	Authority	Page
Pike, James,	Bark. Men,	31
	Rec. Conn. Men,	636
Pike, John, Jr.,	Bark. Men,	31
Priest, Aaron,	Bark. Men,	31
	Rec. Conn. Men,	474
Priest, Darius,	Bark. Men,	32
	Rec. Conn. Men,	291
(Credited to Simsbury; deserted).		
Quamino, Humphrey,	Bark. Men,	32
Ransom, Peletiah,	Bark. Men,	32
	Rec. Conn. Men,	611
(East Haddam).		
Rexford, Joel,	Bark. Men,	32
	Rec. Conn. Men,	471
Rexford, William,	Bark. Men,	32
	Rec. Conn. Men,	17
Rice, Samuel,	Bark. Men,	32
	Rec. Conn. Men,	24, 418, 567
(Two Samuel Rices in the service).		
*Rice, Wait,	Bark. Men,	33
	Pension List,	636
(Came from Wallingford).		
Richardson, Stephen,	Bark. Men,	33
	Rec. Conn. Men,	476
	Rolls and Returns,	145
(At least three of this name in service).		
*Roberts, Judah,	Bark. Men,	33
	Rec. Conn. Men,	541
	Pension List,	653
(Enlisted from Winchester).		
Rockwell, John,	Bark. Men,	33
	Rec. Conn. Men,	17, 583
(Credited to New Hartford. Three John Rockwells in the service).		
*Rogers, Simeon,	Bark. Men,	34
	Rec. Conn. Men,	541
Sanford, Henry,	Bark. Men,	44
	Rec. Conn. Men,	43, 407
(Of Derby).		
*Sanford, Joel,	Bark. Men,	44
	Rec. Conn. Men,	239, 574
(Of Derby).		
*Sanford, Strong,	Bark. Men,	34
	Rec. Conn. Men,	237, 344
	Pension List,	637
(Perhaps served from Derby).		
Shepard, George,	Bark. Men,	34
	Rec. Conn. Men,	471
Shepard, Joseph, Jr.,	Bark. Men,	35
	Rec. Conn. Men,	17
(Three Joseph Shepards in the service).		
Shepard, Moses,	Bark. Men,	35
	Rec. Conn. Men,	35, 60, 625

LITCHFIELD COUNTY REVOLUTIONARY SOLDIERS

Name	Authority	Page
*Slade, Abner,	Bark. Men,	34
	Rec. Conn. Men,	60, 384, 637
(Came from, or near, East Windsor).		
Slade, James,	Bark. Men,	34
	Rec. Conn. Men,	9, 88
*Smith, David,	Bark. Men,	45
	Rec. Conn. Men,	652
(Six David Smiths in the service).		
*Soper, Timothy,	Bark. Men,	44
*Spencer, Thomas,	Bark. Men,	35
	Rec. Conn. Men,	536
	Pension List,	644
(Five Thomas Spencers in the service).		
Squire, David,	Bark. Men,	35
(Two David Squires pensioned in Conn.).		
Tanner, Gideon,	Bark. Men,	35
	Rec. Conn. Men,	259
Taylor, Ebenezer,	Bark. Men,	45
	Rec. Conn. Men,	40
*Taylor, Ozias,	Bark. Men,	45
	Rec. Conn. Men,	495
*Taylor, William, Jr.,	Bark. Men,	36
	Rec. Conn. Men,	21, 50, 159, 335
(Served from Canton. Five William Taylors in the service).		
*Tuttle, Charles,	Bark. Men,	36
	Rec. Conn. Men,	42, 409
*Upson, Saul,	Bark. Men,	36
	Rec. Conn. Men,	382
(Probably served from Wolcott).		
Weed, Jonas,	Lists and Returns,	145
*Whiting, John,	Bark. Men,	37
	Rec. Conn. Men,	203, 546, 652
(Served from Milford. Three, if not four John Whitings in service).		
*Wilcox, Jehiel,	Bark. Men,	37
	Rec. Conn. Men,	341, 637
*Wilcox, Joseph,	Bark. Men,	37
Wilder, Ephraim,	Bark. Men,	37
	Rec. Conn. Men,	17, 471
Wilder, Gamaliel,	Bark. Men,	38
	Rec. Conn. Men,	17
Wilder, John,	Bark. Men,	38
	Rec. Conn. Men,	17, 471
Wilder, Jonathan,	Bark. Men,	38
	Rec. Conn. Men,	61, 471
Wilder, Thomas,	Bark. Men,	38
	Rec. Conn. Men,	540, 638, 652
*Wilson, William,	Bark. Men,	38
*Wood, David,	Bark. Men,	39
	Rec. Conn. Men,	251
(At least four David Woods in the service).		

Name	Authority	Page
Woodruff, Jonah,	Bark. Men,	39
	Rec. Conn. Men,	40
*Wright, Timothy,	Bark. Men,	45
	Rec. Conn. Men,	506

(Served from Colchester).

Canaan

Revolutionary Soldiers

OF

Canaan

COMPILED BY
ROGER SHERMAN CHAPTER
DAUGHTERS OF THE AMERICAN REVOLUTION
NEW MILFORD, CONN.

For fuller accounts of these men see original lists

Revolutionary Soldiers of Canaan

Name	Authority	Page
Austin, Thadeus,	Rec. Conn. Men,	562
Bailey, Henry,	Rec. Conn. Men,	583
Baker, Ozias,	Lists and Returns,	63
Barnes, John,	Lists and Returns,	279
Bayley, Thomas,	Rec. Conn. Men,	562
Beebe, David,	Lists and Returns,	279
Belding, Joshua,	Rec. Conn. Men,	562
Benedict, James,	D. A. R. Lin. Book Vol. XXII.,	9
Benton, Caleb,	Rec. Conn. Men,	208
Bishop, Joseph,	Lists and Returns,	211
Bishop, Richard,	Lists and Returns,	46, 63
Blinn, Jonathan,	Rec. Conn. Men,	278
Bolden, Joshua,	Rec. Conn. Men,	664
Brownel, Aaron, Sergt.,	Lists and Returns,	63, 64
Burrall, Charles, Col.,	Rec. Conn. Men,	110, 437
	D. A. R. Lin. Book Vol. XXIII.,	221
Burrall, Jonathan, (Dep. Paymaster, Cincinnati),	Rec. Conn. Men,	313
Butler, Benjamin,	Lists and Returns,	208
Camp, John,	Rec. Conn. Men,	280
Cande, Zacheus,	Lists and Returns,	208
Carter, John,	D. A. R. Lin. Book Vol. XXV.,	188
Chambers, William,	Lists and Returns,	25, 63, 236
Church, Ebenezer,	Lists and Returns,	63
Clary, James,	Rec. Conn. Men,	216
Cogswell, Asa,	Lists and Returns,	211
Coole, Himan,	Lists and Returns,	63
Cowles, Joseph,	Lists and Returns,	46, 63
Cowles, Timothy,	D. A. R. Lin. Book Vol. XIII.,	334
Culver, Aaron,	Rec. Conn. Men,	221
	Gen. Huntington's Note Book. Lists and Returns,	25, 63, 236
Curtis, Seth,	Lists and Returns,	46, 63
	Rec. Conn. Men,	583
Curtiss, Giles,	Lists and Returns,	207
Curtiss, John,	Rolls and Lists Vol. VIII.,	23
	Lists and Returns,	46, 63
Daily, Obadiah,	Rec. Conn. Men,	276
Douglas, John,	D. A. R. Lin. Book Vol. XV., Died in New York.	3
Douglas, Nathaniel,	Lists and Returns,	63

LITCHFIELD COUNTY REVOLUTIONARY SOLDIERS

Name	Authority	Page
Dunham, Cornelius,	Lists and Returns,	211
Dunham, David,	Lists and Returns,	189
Dunham, Gideon,	Lists and Returns,	206
Dunham, Thomas,	Rec. Conn. Men,	583
Emmonds, Jonathan,	Lists and Returns,	206
Fellows, Abiel,	D. A. R. Lin. Book Vol. XXII.,	109
Fellows, David, Ensign,	Rec. Conn. Men,	260
Fellows, Ephraim,	D. A. R. Lin. Book Vol. XXVII.,	242
Fellows, William, Corp.,	Rec. Conn. Men,	219
	Lists and Returns,	63
Fenn, Theophilus, Capt.,	Grave marked by S. A. R.	
Freeman, Elisha,	Lists and Returns,	28, 63, 236
Fuller, Eleazur,	App. for Pension.	
Furbs, ———, Corp.,	Rec. Conn. Men,	583
Gale, Christopher,	Rec. Conn. Men,	275
Gillett, Jonathan,	Rec. Conn. Men,	664
Green, Samuel,	Lists and Returns,	29, 63, 236
Grizwold, Warren,	Lists and Returns,	46
Hamilton, Samuel,	Rec. Conn. Men,	570
Handford, Austin,	Rec. Conn. Men,	362
Harrison, Czar,	Rec. Conn. Men,	583
Hewitt, Gersham, Capt.,	Rec. Conn. Men,	616, 653
	Spy Ticonderoga.	
Hide, Asa,	Lists and Returns,	211, 279
Higby, Elihu,	Lists and Returns,	30, 236
Higby, Isaac,	Lists and Returns,	63
	Rec. Conn. Men,	223
Hinman, Joseph,	Rolls and Lists,	52
Holcomb, Abraham,	Rec. Conn. Men,	664
Holombeck, John, Lieut.,	Lists and Returns,	63, 236
Hunt, Russell, Sergt.,	Rec. Conn. Men,	219
	Lists and Returns,	63
Hunt, Samson, R.,	Lists and Returns,	46
Hunt, Samuel.	Lists and Returns,	63
Hunt, Solomon,	Rec. Conn. Men,	583
Jakeway, Daniel,	App. for Pension.	
Johnson, Joseph,	Lists and Returns,	279
Johnson, Timothy,	Rec. Conn. Men,	562
Jonathan, Gideon,	Lists and Returns,	279
Jones, David,	Lists and Returns,	279
Jones, Squire,	Rec. Conn. Men,	275
Jones, Stephen,	Gen. Jedekiah Huntington's Note Book.	
Judd, Thomas,	Rec. Conn. Men,	664
Kimball, Jesse, Capt.,	Rec. Conn. Men,	230
Knap, Lemuel,	Rec. Conn. Men,	562
Lawrence, Asa,	Rec. Conn. Men,	562
Lawrence, Bille,	Lists and Returns,	46, 63
Lawrence, Elijah,	Rec. Conn. Men,	259

CANAAN

Name	Authority	Page
Lawrence, John,	Lists and Returns,	228
Lawrence, Nehemiah,	Rec. Conn. Men,	117
Lee, Elias, Sergt.,	Lists and Returns,	46, 63
Lester, Andrew,	Lists and Returns,	63, 236
McNiel, Niel, Corp.,	Rec. Conn. Men,	266
	Lists and Returns,	63
Merrills, Medad,	Rec. Conn. Men,	213
*Merrils, Nathaniel,	Rec. Conn. Men,	664
Miller, Abner,	Lists and Returns,	46, 63
Mitchell, John,	Rec. Conn. Men,	259
Mix, William,	Lists and Returns,	46, 63
Pardy, Ebenezer,	Lists and Returns,	207
Pierce, Samuel,	Lists and Returns,	63
Porridge, Samuel,	Lists and Returns,	279
Prindle, Ezra,	Rec. Conn. Men,	259
Preston, Asa,	Rec. Conn. Men,	562
Preston, Davis,	Lists and Returns,	46, 63
Prevett, John,	Lists and Returns,	63
Onkshun, John,	Lists and Returns,	279
Ranson, Samuel,	Rec. Conn. Men,	261
Root, Joshua,	Lists and Returns,	202, 211
Root, Nathaniel,	Rolls and Lists Vol. VIII.,	55
	D. A. R. Lin. Book Vol. XXVI.,	278
Rose, John, Ensign,	Rec. Conn. Men,	257
Rose, William,	Lists and Returns,	214
Scovil, Benjamin,	Lists and Returns,	63
Serdam, Peter,	Lists and Returns,	63
Smith, Isaac,	Lists and Returns,	46, 63
Smith, William,	App. for Pension.	
Spaulding, Ariel,	Rec. Conn. Men,	563
Stephens, Benjamin,	App. for Pension.	
Stevens, John, Capt.,	Rec. Conn. Men,	111
Stevens, Stephen,	Lists and Returns,	46, 63
Stevens, Thomas,	Lists and Returns,	46, 63
St. John, Gideon,	Lists and Returns,	189
Stoddard, Luther, Capt.,	Rec. Conn. Men,	110
Studson, Thomas,	Lists and Returns,	279
Tubbs, Simon,	Rec. Conn. Men,	299
	Lists and Returns,	46, 63
Wallen, James,	Rec. Conn. Men,	562
Watrous, James, Q. M.,	Rec. Conn. Men,	63
Watson, John, Jr., Capt.,	Rec. Conn. Men,	63
	Rolls and Lists Vol. VIII.,	22
	Lists and Returns,	63
	See Goshen List.	
Wentworth, Gibbon,	Rolls and Lists Vol. VIII.,	21
Wheedon, Jeremiah,	Lists and Returns,	279
White, George,	Lists and Returns,	211

Name	Authority	Page
Whitney, Jonathan, Capt.,	Rec. Conn. Men,	485
Whitney, Josiah,	Rolls and Lists Vol. VIII.,	21
Whitney, Joshua, Lieut.,	Rec. Conn. Men,	230, 345
	Lists and Returns,	46, 63
	D. A. R. Lin. Book Vol. XXVI.,	105
Whitney, Tarbell, Capt.,	Rec. Conn. Men,	313
Williams, Samuel,	Rolls and Lists Vol. VIII.,	21
Williams, Thomas, Lieut.,	App. for Pension.	
Woodford, Timothy,	Lists and Returns,	63

Colebrook

Revolutionary Soldiers

OF

Colebrook

COMPILED BY
GREEN WOODS CHAPTER
DAUGHTERS OF THE AMERICAN REVOLUTION
WINSTED, CONN.

For fuller accounts of these men see original lists

Revolutionary Soldiers of Colebrook

Name	Authority	Page
Bass, Nathan,	Rec. Conn. Men, Year Book S. A. R.	17, 471
Bidwell, Eleazar,	Rec. Conn. Men, Ms. Hist. Colebrook,	663
*Canfield, Abriel,	Rec. Conn. Men, Lists and Returns,	197 65, 235
*Copps, David,	Rec. Conn. Men,	633
*Corbin, Peter, Capt.,	Boyd's Annals. Lists and Returns,	361
*Corbin, Peter Jr.,	Rec. Conn. Men, Has Marker.	583
*Cowles, Dea. Samuel,	Rec. Conn. Men,	18
*Deming, Daniel,	Rec. Conn. Men,	25, 51, 498
*De Wolf, Daniel,	Rec. Conn. Men,	568
Griswold, Aaron,	Rec. Conn. Men,	471
Griswold, Francis,	Rec. Conn. Men,	416
*Hart, Titus,	Rec. Conn. Men,	634, 653, 663
*Hudson, George (Hutson),	Rec. Conn. Men, Boyd's Annals,	259 162
*Marshall, Elijah,	Rec. Conn. Men, 92, 630, 635, Stiles "Ancient Windsor" Vol. I.,	666 362
*Mills, David,	Buried in Colebrook River.	
Mills, Pelatiah,	Rec. Conn. Men, Ms. Hist. Colebrook.	536
Mills, Samuel,	Rec. Conn. Men, Manual Cong. Church.	17
*Orvis, David,	Rec. Conn. Men, Cressey's Norfolk,	18, 653, 663 87
*Phelps, Asah,	Inscription on stone.	
*Phelps, Daniel,	Rec. Conn. Men,	623
*Phelps, John,	Rec. Conn. Men,	652, 669
Phillips, Samuel,	Ms. Hist. Colebrook. Lists and Returns,	65, 235
Pinney, David,	Rec. Conn. Men, Ms. Hist. Colebrook.	17
Porter, John,	Rec. Conn. Men, Ms. Hist. Colebrook.	471
Riley, Phillip,	Lists and Returns,	269
*Roberts, Paul,	Stiles Windsor Vol. I.,	368
Rockwell, David, Corp.,	Rec. Conn. Men, Hist. Colebrook.	499

Name	Authority	Page
Rockwell, Elijah,	Rec. Conn. Men,	471
Rockwell, Gurdon,	Rec. Conn. Men,	499
	Ms. Hist. Colebrook.	
Rockwell, John,	Rec. Conn. Men,	17, 396
	Ms. Hist. Colebrook.	
Rockwell, Joseph,	Cressey's Norfolk.	
	Lists and Returns,	206
Rockwell, Samuel,	Rec. Conn. Men,	548
Rockwell, Samuel, Jr.,	Rec. Conn. Men,	653
	Stiles Windsor Vol. II.,	652
	Ms. Hist. Colebrook.	
*Rogers, Josiah,	Rec. Conn. Men,	7, 50
*Sage, Enos,	Rec. Conn. Men,	653
*Sage, Stephen,	Rec. Conn. Men,	48
Sharp, Isaac,	Rec. Conn. Men,	627
Shepherd, Ebenezer,	Rec. Conn. Men,	471
	Ms. Hist. Colebrook.	
	Boyd's Annals,	266
Simons, Eli,	Lists and Returns,	40, 175, 235
Simons, Hezekiah, Corp.,	Rec. Conn. Men,	471
Simons, Joseph,	Lists and Returns,	65, 235
Simons, William,	Rec. Conn. Men,	17
*Taylor, Jesse,	App. Pension.	
	Rec. Conn. Men,	663, 637
	Ms. Hist. Colebrook.	
*Thomas, John,	Rec. Conn. Men,	663
*Wakefield, Pattershall,	Stiles Windsor Vol. I.,	372
	Lists and Returns,	241
*White, Ephraim,	Rec. Conn. Men,	663
	App. Pension.	
*Williams, Obed,	Rec. Conn. Men,	238
	App. Pension.	
Wilmer, John,	Rec. Conn. Men,	259
Wright, Moses,	Rec. Conn. Men,	167

Cornwall

Revolutionary Soldiers

OF

Cornwall

PRESENTED, IN PART, BY
JUDEA CHAPTER
DAUGHTERS OF THE AMERICAN REVOLUTION
WASHINGTON, CONN.

REVISED BY
MARY FLOYD TALLMADGE CHAPTER
DAUGHTERS OF THE AMERICAN REVOLUTION
LITCHFIELD, CONN.

For fuller accounts of these men see original lists

Revolutionary Soldiers of Cornwall

Name	Authority	Page
Abbot, Abel,	Rec. Conn. Men,	562
Allen, Daniel,	Rec. Conn. Men,	420
Allen, Ebenezer,	Rec. Conn. Men,	629
Allen, Edward, Corp.,	Rec. Conn. Men, Hist. of Cornwall,	363, 627 221
*Allen, Gen. Ethan,	Litchfield List.	
*Allen, Heber, Major,	Hist. Cornwall,	450
*Allen, Heman, Capt.,	Salisbury.	
*Allen, Ira, Col.,	Rec. Conn. Men,	32
Allen, Joseph,	Rec. Conn. Men,	420
Andrews, Hezekiah, Lieut.,	Rec. Conn. Men,	395
Avery, Abel,	Rec. Conn. Men,	395, 664
Avery, William,	Rec. Conn. Men,	396
*Baldwin, Henry,	Hist. Cornwall, App. for Pension.	275, 445
Baldwin, Samuel,	Lists and Returns,	204
Beach, Elnathan,	Rolls and Lists, Rec. Conn. Men, Lists and Returns,	55 420 207
Bell, Jonathan,	Rolls and Lists,	274
Bell, Kitchel, Jr.,	Hist. Cornwall,	207
Bierce, William, Sergt.,	Hist. Cornwall,	221
Boney, Pierce, (Perez)	Rolls and Lists, Lists and Returns,	56 47
Bonney, Jairus,	Hist. Cornwall,	251
Bradford, Elisha, Corp.,	Conn. Men, Hist. Cornwall,	220 221
Bristol, Nathaniel,	Rec. Conn. Men,	62, 397
Brown, Francis,	Rec. Conn. Men, Hist. Cornwall,	290 206
Brown, Ichabod,	Rec. Conn. Men, Hist. Cornwall,	396 206
Brownell, Aaron,	Rec. Conn. Men, (Canaan).	397
*Brownson, Elisha,	Rec. Conn. Men,	423
Burnham, Oliver,	Hist. Cornwall,	216
Burton, Samuel,	Rolls and Lists,	274
Camp, Abel,	Rec. Conn. Men, D. A. R. Lin. Book Vol. V.,	574 109
Carrier, Benjamin,	Rec. Conn. Men,	397
Carter, John, Sergt.,	Hist. Cornwall,	207
Carter, John 1st.,	Rec. Conn. Men,	366

68 LITCHFIELD COUNTY REVOLUTIONARY SOLDIERS

Name	Authority	Page
Catlin, Bradley,	Rolls and Lists,	201
	Conn. Men,	502
*Chandler, Benjamin,	Rec. Conn. Men,	304
*Chandler, John, (Newtown)	Rec. Conn. Men,	229
Chickster, William,	Hist. Cornwall,	221
Clany, Luke,	Rec. Conn. Men,	583
Clark, George,	Rec. Conn. Men,	664
Clark, Hezekiah,	Not found.	
Clark, Silas,	Rec. Conn. Men,	364, 370
	Hist. Cornwall,	207
Coe, Andrew,	Rec. Conn. Men,	397
Cole, James,	Rec. Conn. Men,	562
Coles, David, (N. Milford),	Rec. Conn. Men,	363
Cook, William, Corp.,	Rec. Conn. Men,	221
Cook, ———,	Rec. Conn. Men,	365
Coon, Daniel,	Rec. Conn. Men,	397
Corhoy, (or Chrisdroy),	Rec. Conn. Men,	63, 396
Cowl, Asa,	Rec. Conn. Men,	397
Dandrig, Samuel, Sergt.,	Rec. Conn. Men,	397
Darrow, Samuel,	Rec. Conn. Men,	397
Dean, Reuben,	App. for Pension.	
	Rec. Conn. Men,	222
	Hist. Cornwall,	221
Dean, Samuel,	Rec. Conn. Men,	569
	Lists and Returns,	207
Demonia, John,	Rec. Conn. Men,	397
Dibble, Benjamin,	Rec. Conn. Men,	583
	Lists and Returns,	211
Dibble, Israel,	Rec. Conn. Men,	647
	Hist. Cornwall,	453
	Rolls and Lists,	274
Dibble, John,	Hist. Cornwall,	207
Dibble, John 4th.,	Hist. Cornwall,	207
Dibble, Silas,	Lists and Returns,	47
Dooty, Timothy,	Rec. Conn. Men,	397
Dormon, Gershom,	Rec. Conn. Men,	397
Douglas, David,	Rec. Conn. Men,	397
Doyle, James,	Rec. Conn. Men,	397
Dusumer, Elisha,	Rolls and Lists,	274
Emmons, Asa,	Rolls and Lists,	274
Emmons, Salmon,	Hist. Cornwall,	249
Emmons, Samuel,	Rolls and Lists,	274
Emmons, Solomon,	Rec. Conn. Men,	397
Forbes, Elijah,	Rec. Conn. Men,	397
Ford, Allyn,	Not found.	
Ford, Hezekiah, Sergt.,	Rec. Conn. Men,	420
Fox, Allen,	Rec. Conn. Men,	63, 222
Fox, Reuben,	Rec. Conn. Men,	579

CORNWALL 69

Name	Authority	Page
Franklin, David,	Rec. Conn. Men,	396
Franklin, Samuel,	Rec. Conn. Men,	396
Freedom, Jack,	Rec. Conn. Men,	327
	Lists and Returns,	277
Fuller, Rosel,	Rec. Conn. Men,	397
George, Moses,	Lists and Returns,	277
Gibbs, Oliver,	Rolls and Lists,	55
Gillet, Lemuel,	Rec. Conn. Men,	63, 396
Grimes, Abraham,	Rolls and Lists,	56
	Lists and Returns,	47
Guest, John,	Rec. Conn. Men,	634
	App. for Pension.	
Hamlin, Thomas,	Rec. Conn. Men,	397
Hand, Abraham, Sergt. and Lieut.,	Rec. Conn. Men,	291
Harrik, Ephriam,	Rec. Conn. Men,	397
Harris, Daniel,	Rec. Conn. Men,	397
Harris, Israel,	D. A. R. Lin. Book Vol. XXII.,	107
Harrison, Joseph,	Hist. Cornwall,	420
Harrison, Noah,	Rolls and Lists,	274
Hart, Elias, Capt.,	Hist. Cornwall,	307
Hart, John,	Rec. Conn. Men,	420
Hart, Lot,	Hist. Cornwall,	307
	Rec. Conn. Men,	63
Hart, Phineas,	Hist. Cornwall,	307
Hart, Thomas,	Rolls and Lists,	55, 274
Hartshorn, Joshua,	Rolls and Lists,	274, 221
	Lists and Returns,	47
Heth, a slave of Mr. Wadsworth,	Hist. Cornwall,	221
Highcock, David,	Rec. Conn. Men,	397
Hopkins, Josiah,	Rolls and Lists,	274
Hotchkiss, Joseph,	Rec. Conn. Men,	420
Howe, Deliverence,	Rec. Conn. Men,	362
*Hull, Zephaniah,	Rec. Conn. Men,	282, 634
	App. for Pension.	
(Enlisted from Wallingford.)		
Jacaway, William,	Rec. Conn. Men,	397
Jackson, Joel,	Rec. Conn. Men,	397
Jeffers, John, Sergt.,	Rec. Conn. Men,	362
Jeffry, Rolin,	Lists and Returns,	277
Jennings, Bennett,	App. for Pension.	
	Rec. Conn. Men,	664
Johnson, Amos, Jr., Sergt.,	Hist. Cornwall,	253
Johnson, Solomon,	Rec. Conn. Men,	227
	Rolls and Lists,	274
	Lists and Returns,	208
*Johnson, Timothy, (Canaan)	Rec. Conn. Men,	562

LITCHFIELD COUNTY REVOLUTIONARY SOLDIERS

Name	Authority	Page
Judd, Samuel,	D. A. R. Lin. Book Vol. XX.,	50
Kellogg, Solomon, (Killingly)	Rec. Conn. Men,	627
Knap, Elnathan, (Sharon),	Rec. Conn. Men,	397
Knapp, Timothy, Sergt.,	Rec. Conn. Men,	397
	Hist. Cornwall,	206
Lake, Phineas,	Rec. Conn. Men,	397
Lampson, Samuel,	Rec. Conn. Men,	224
	Lists and Returns,	33, 171
Lawrence, David,	Rec. Conn. Men,	397
Lazell, Abner,	Rolls and Returns,	277
Leet, Asahel,	Rolls and Lists,	274
Lindley, Joseph,	Rolls and Lists,	74
Mallory, David,	Rec. Conn. Men,	664
	App. for Pension.	
Mebbins, John,	Rolls and Lists,	274
Millard, Charles,	D. A. R. Lin. Book Vol. XVII.,	151
	Lists and Returns,	206
North, Simeon,	Rolls and Lists,	274
Odle, William,	Rec. Conn. Men,	653
Pangborn, Adonijah,	Rec. Conn. Men,	664
Pangborn, Beebe,	Rec. Conn. Men,	562
	Lists and Returns,	206
Pardee, Ebenezer,	Rec. Conn. Men,	397
Pardee, Gamaliel,	Rec. Conn. Men,	397
Parmalee, Joshua,	Rec. Conn. Men,	396, 397
Patterson, John,	Rec. Conn. Men,	420
Patterson, Sherman, Sergt.,	Hist. of Cornwall,	207
Patterson, William, Lieut.,	Rec. Conn. Men,	61, 110
Payne, Barnabas,	Rec. Conn. Men,	113
Payne, Rev. Abraham,	Hist. of Cornwall,	207, 231
Payne, Rufus, Sergt.,	Hist. of Cornwall,	207
	App. for Pension.	
Peck, Stephen,	App. for Pension.	
Perry, Ezekiel,	Rec. Conn. Men,	63
Philemor, Henry,	Rolls and Lists,	274
Pierce, Benjamin,	Rec. Conn. Men,	420
Pierce, Joseph, Sergt.,	Rec. Conn. Men,	276
Pierce, Joshua, Capt.,	Hist. of Cornwall,	207
Pierce, Levi,	Rolls and Lists,	90
	Lists and Returns,	36
Pierce, William, Corp.,	Rec. Conn. Men,	420
Potter, Daniel,	Rec. Conn. Men,	397
Pratt, Joseph,	App. for Pension.	
Pratt, Peter,	Rec. Conn. Men,	397
Rogers, Edward, Capt.,	Rec. Conn. Men,	614
	D. A. R. Lin. Book Vol. XVIII.,	253
	Hist. of Cornwall,	205, 207

CORNWALL

Name	Authority	Page
Rogers, Noah,	Hist. of Cornwall,	202
	D. A. R. Lin. Book Vol. XX.,	18
Rowley, Timothy,	Rec. Conn. Men,	397
Rowlin, Luke,	Rec. Conn. Men,	397
Russ, Epaphras, Corp.,	Rec. Conn. Men,	225
	Lists and Returns,	173, 269
Schofield, Joseph,	Rolls and Lists,	55
Scoville, Jacob,	Rec. Conn. Men,	583, 664
	App. for Pension.	
Scoville, Samuel,	Hist. of Cornwall,	259
Scoville, Samuel, Jr.,	Lists and Returns,	277
Sedgwick, John, Major,	Rec. Conn. Men,	61, 110
	Hist. of Cornwall,	210
	D. A. R. Lin. Book Vol. II.,	294
Shipman, William,	Rec. Conn. Men,	63
Simmons, David,	Rec. Conn. Men,	397
Simmons, Samuel,	Record in Pension Dept.	
	Lists and Returns,	40
Slade, William,	Rec. Conn. Men,	63
Smith, Asa,	Rec. Conn. Men,	397
Smith, Nehemiah,	Rec. Conn. Men,	397
Squire, Jonathan,	Rec. Conn. Men,	286
Steele, Elijah,	Rec. Conn. Men,	41
Steele, Matthew M.,	Rec. Conn. Men,	361
Sterling, James,	Rec. Conn. Men,	397
	Hist. of Cornwall,	206
Stow, Deliverance,	Lists and Returns,	277
Surdam, Samuel,	Rec. Conn. Men,	397
Swift, Heman, Capt.,	Rec. Conn. Men,	368
	Hist. of Cornwall,	213
	Lists and Returns,	40
Swift, Isaac, Surgeon,	Rec. Conn. Men,	217
Tanner, Ebenezer, Lieut.,	Rec. Conn. Men,	323, 375
Tanner, Joseph A.,	Rec. Conn. Men,	226
	Hist. of Cornwall,	221
Tanner, Thomas, Lieut.,	Rec. Conn. Men,	414
	D. A. R. Lin. Book Vol. XX.,	134
Tanner, Tyral (Loyal), Lieut.,	Rec Conn. Men,	113
	Lists and Returns,	42, 88
Toole, Peter,	Rec. Conn. Men,	397
Trowbridge, Joel,	Hist. of Cornwall,	446
Trowbridge, Stephen, Sergt.,	D. A. R. Lin. Book Vol. XX.,	231
Wadsworth, James,	Rolls and Lists,	274
Wagner, Adam,	Rec. Conn. Men,	397
Waller, Ashbel,	Rolls and Lists,	56
Walter, Seth,	Rec. Conn. Men,	570
Warrups, Thomas,	Lists and Returns,	103
	Hist. of Cornwall,	24
	See Kent List.	

Name	Authority	Page
Weeks (Wix), Uriah (Beriah), Sergt.,	Rec. Conn. Men,	364
Weeks, Zepheniah,	Not found.	
West, Joseph,	Rec. Conn. Men,	583
White, Eli,	Rolls and Lists,	56
White, John,	Rec. Conn. Men,	397
	Hist. of Cornwall,	206
White, John Jr.,	Rec. Conn. Men,	397
White, Thomas,	Rolls and Lists,	274
*Whitney, Asa,	Rec. Conn. Men, Salisbury.	93
Whitney, David,	Rec. Conn. Men,	397
Williams, Uriah,	Rec. Conn. Men,	397
Wilson, James,	Hist. of Cornwall,	206
Wise, Uriah (Wix),	Rolls and Lists,	91
	Lists and Returns,	43
Young, Ebenezer,	Rec. Conn. Men,	327
Young, Jacob,	Lists and Returns,	277

Goshen

Revolutionary Soldiers

OF

Goshen

COMPILED BY
TORRINGTON CHAPTER
DAUGHTERS OF THE AMERICAN REVOLUTION
TORRINGTON, CONN.

For fuller accounts of these men see original lists

Revolutionary Soldiers of Goshen

Name	Authority	Page
Andrews, Theodore,	Hist. Goshen,	153, 118
	Rec. Conn. Men,	247
Andro, Gideon,	Rec. Conn. Men,	562
Baily, Andrew,	Hist. Goshen,	136
	Rec. Conn. Men,	612
Baldwin, Brenin,	Hist. Goshen,	153
	Rec. Conn. Men,	652
Baldwin, Daniel,	Rec. Conn. Men,	612, 654
Baldwin, Isaac,	Hist. Goshen,	153
	Rec. Conn. Men,	232, 513, 549, 628
	D. A. R. Lin. Book Vol. XXIII.,	59
(More than one, it seems, in the service).		
Baldwin, Samuel,	Hist. Goshen,	153
	Rec. Conn. Men,	81, 203, 382
Bartholemew, Isaac,	Hist. Goshen,	415
	Rec. Conn. Men,	641
Bartholemew, Josiah, Jr.,	Hist. Goshen,	128
Bartholemew, Moses,	Hist. Goshen,	415
	Rolls and Lists,	275
	Rec. Conn. Men,	615
Bartholemew, Oliver,	Hist. Goshen,	415
Bartholemew, Samuel,	Hist. Goshen,	415
	Rec. Conn. Men,	345, 531, 633
Bassett, Abel,	Lists and Returns,	69
Beach, Abraham,	Hist. Goshen,	424, 127
Beach, Ambrose,	Rec. Conn. Men,	62
Beach, Amos,	Hist. Goshen,	136, 424
	Rec. Conn. Men,	63
Beach, Ashbel,	Hist. Goshen,	131
	Rolls and Lists,	20
Beach, Bruen,	Lists and Returns,	204
Beach, Edmund,	Hist. Goshen,	118, 127
	Rec. Conn. Men,	549
Beach, Fisk,	Hist. Goshen,	136
	Rec. Conn. Men,	612
Beach, Israel,	Hist. Goshen,	120, 153
	Rec. Conn. Men,	641
Beach, John,	Hist. Goshen,	120, 153
Beach, Jonathan,	Rec. Conn. Men,	562, 570
	D. A. R. Lin. Book Vol. XXV.,	3, 4
Beach, Julius,	Hist. Goshen,	154
	Rec. Conn. Men,	327, 363, 652
	Lists and Returns,	275

Name	Authority	Page
Beach, Martin,	Hist. Goshen,	127
	Rec. Conn. Men,	397
Beach, Medad,	Hist. Goshen,	154
Beach, Obed,	Hist. Goshen,	154
Beach, Obil,	Rec. Conn. Men,	646
	Lists and Returns,	69
Beach, Rice,	Lists and Returns,	206
Becklee, Zobed,	Hist. Goshen,	154
	Rec. Conn. Men,	583
Benton, Adoniram,	Lists and Returns,	185
Bingham, Thamer,	Lists and Returns,	206
Boney, Javis,	Lists and Returns,	69
Brooks, Asa,	Hist. Goshen,	128, 154
	Rec. Conn. Men,	196, 502, 641
	Lists and Returns,	69
Brooks, Joseph,	Hist. Goshen,	142, 154
	Rec. Conn. Men,	481
	Rolls and Lists,	22
Brown, James,	Hist. Goshen,	128, 136
	Rec. Conn. Men,	612, 63, 83
	Lists and Returns,	69
Buckley, Matthew,	Lists and Returns,	69
Buel, Jonathan,	Hist. Goshen,	438, 154, 138
	Rec. Conn. Men,	502
(Another Jonathan Buel of Litchfield).		
Buel, Jonathan, Jr.,	Hist. Goshen,	438, 136
	Rolls and Lists,	37
Buell, Timothy,	Hist. Goshen,	440, 118, 127
Butler, Abel,	Hist. Goshen,	154
	Rec. Conn. Men,	63, 196
	Rolls and Lists,	39
Butler, Abel, Jr.,	Rolls and Lists,	22
Butler, Joseph,	Hist. Goshen,	120, 154
	Rolls and Lists,	39
Carr, Caleb,	Hist. Goshen,	154, 126
	Rec. Conn. Men,	209
Carr, John,	Hist. Goshen,	154, 126
	Rec. Conn. Men,	62, 397
Carrington, John,	Hist. Goshen,	136
	Rec. Conn. Men,	612
Carter, Nathan,	Hist. Goshen,	120, 154
	Rec. Conn. Men,	328
	Lists and Returns,	263, 275
Castle, Thomas,	Hist. Goshen,	154
Caswell, Ezra,	Hist. Goshen,	154
	Rec. Conn. Men,	361, 640
	Lists and Returns,	263
Catlin, Elisha,	Hist. Goshen,	136
	Rec. Conn. Men,	612
	Rolls and Lists,	202

GOSHEN 79

Name	Authority	Page
Chapin, Ichabod,	Hist. Goshen,	127, 154
	Rec. Conn. Men,	228
	Rolls and Lists,	202
	Lists and Returns,	209
Collins, Ambrose,	Hist. Goshen,	120, 142
	Rec. Conn. Men,	653
	Rolls and Lists,	37
*Collins, Cyprian,	Hist. Goshen,	143, 154
	Lists and Returns,	274
	D. A. R. Lin. Book Vol. XXIII.,	307
Collins, Philo,	Hist. Goshen,	154
Converse, Thomas,	Hist. Goshen,	120, 152
	Rec. Conn. Men,	375
	Rolls and Lists,	33, 37, 48
	Lists and Returns,	26, 69, 165, 235
Cook, Amasa,	Rec. Conn. Men,	612
Crane, James,	Rec. Conn. Men,	336, 542
	Rolls and Lists,	102
	Lists and Returns,	275
Davis, James,	Hist. Goshen,	127
	Rec. Conn. Men,	63
Davis, Joel,	Hist. Goshen,	127, 154
	Rec. Conn. Men,	155
Deane, Jonathan,	Lists and Returns,	274
Dear, George,	Hist. Goshen,	118
	Rolls and Lists,	37
	Goshen Statistics,	44
Dear, George, Jr.,	Hist. Goshen,	127
	Rec. Conn. Men,	197, 502, 549
	Rolls and Lists,	22
Dear, John,	Goshen Statistics,	247
Dear, John, Jr.,	Goshen Statistics,	247
	Rec. Conn. Men,	365, 642
Deming, Jonathan,	Hist. Goshen,	118
	Rec. Conn. Men,	203, 218, 323, 639
	Rolls and Lists,	39
	Lists and Returns,	69
Deming, Wait, (Wail)	Lists and Returns,	27, 69, 235
Dickinson, Thomas,	Rec. Conn. Men,	562
	D. A. R. Lin. Book Vol. XXV.,	168
Dill, Martin,	Lists and Returns,	205
Doud, John,	Goshen Statistics,	253
	Hist. Goshen,	136
	Rec. Conn. Men,	612
	Rolls and Lists,	38
Fields, Robert,	Lists and Returns,	203
Francis, Asa,	Goshen Statistics,	265
	Hist. Goshen,	152
Francis, David,	Rec. Conn. Men,	365
	Lists and Returns,	274
Gardner, George,	Lists and Returns,	69

Name	Authority	Page
Gaylord, Joel,	Hist. Goshen,	136
	Rec. Conn. Men,	138, 612
	Rolls and Lists,	97, 139, 222
	Lists and Returns,	69
Gaylord, Joseph,	Hist. Goshen,	154
	Rec. Conn. Men,	653
	Rolls and Lists,	139
Gaylord, Titus,	Hist. Goshen,	154
Goodwin, Stephen,	Hist. Goshen,	152
	Rec. Conn. Men,	395
	Goshen Statistics,	279
Goodwin, Stephen, Jr.,	Hist. Goshen,	153
	Rolls and Lists,	39
Gould, John,	Goshen Statistics,	278
	Rec. Conn. Men,	198, 636
	Rolls and Lists,	68, 199
	Lists and Returns,	30, 69, 168, 235
Grant, John,	Hist. Goshen,	136
	Rec. Conn. Men,	612
Griswold, Alexander,	Hist. Goshen,	154
Griswold, Oliver,	Hist. Goshen,	127
Hale, Adino,	Hist. Goshen,	126
Hale, Justus,	Hist. Goshen,	154
	Rec. Conn. Men,	228
	Lists and Returns,	209
Hall, Asaph,	Rec. Conn. Men,	61
	Rolls and Lists,	203
Hall, Simeon, (deceased)	Lists and Returns,	50, 69
Hart, David,	Hist. Goshen,	154
Hayden, Samuel,	Goshen Statistics,	299
	Hist. Goshen,	118, 154
	Rolls and Lists,	22
	Rec. Conn. Men,	459
Hayden, Seth,	Hist. Goshen,	118, 120, 154
	Rolls and Lists,	39
Haylord, Joel,	Rec. Conn. Men,	363
Hills, Augustus,	Goshen Statistics,	318
	Rec. Conn. Men,	181
Hills, Medad,	Hist. Goshen,	152
	Rec. Conn. Men,	438, 612
	Rolls and Lists,	225
	D. A. R. Lin. Book Vol. XXV.,	227
Hills, Seth,	Hist. Goshen,	120, 154
	Rec. Conn. Men,	37
Hills, Uri,	Goshen Statistics,	314
	Hist. Goshen,	154
	Rec. Conn. Men,	203
	Lists and Returns,	206
Hinman, Lewis,	Goshen Statistics,	327
	Hist. Goshen,	128, 154
	Rolls and Lists,	37
Hinman, Phineas,	Hist. Goshen,	136
	Rec. Conn. Men,	612

GOSHEN

Name	Authority	Page
Hobbs, John,	Hist. Goshen,	118, 154
	Rec. Conn. Men,	123, 413
Holmes, David,	Hist. Goshen,	129, 154
	Rec. Conn. Men,	223, 640
	Lists and Returns,	69
Hopkins, Samuel,	Hist. Goshen,	136
	Rec. Conn. Men,	612
Howe, Jaazaniah,	Goshen Statistics,	270
	Hist. Goshen,	154
	Rec. Conn. Men,	195, 647
	Rolls and Lists,	68, 269
Hoy, John,	Hist. Goshen,	154
Humphrey, Charles,	Hist. Goshen,	154
	Rec. Conn. Men,	495
Humphrey, David,	Hist. Goshen,	127, 154
Humphrey, Simeon,	Hist. Goshen,	127, 154
	Rolls and Lists,	202
Hunt, William,	Hist. Goshen,	154
	Rec. Conn. Men,	258, 328
Hurlbut, Cyprian,	Rec. Conn. Men,	259, 328, 352
Hurlbut, David,	Hist. Goshen,	154
	Rec. Conn. Men,	219, 643
	Lists and Returns,	69
Hurlbut, Ephraim,	Rec. Conn. Men,	627
Hurlbut, Jeremiah,	Hist. Goshen,	118, 120
	Rec. Conn. Men,	63
	Rolls and Lists,	20
Ingraham, Abner,	Hist. Goshen,	154
	Rec. Conn. Men,	583
Ives, Benjamin,	Hist. Goshen,	136
	Rec. Conn. Men,	571, 612
Jones, Jared,	Hist. Goshen,	136
	Rec. Conn. Men,	612
Judd, Jesse,	Hist. Goshen,	126, 152
	Rec. Conn. Men,	395
	D. A. R. Lin. Book Vol. XXV.,	262
Kellogg, Bradford,	Hist. Goshen,	138, 154
	Rolls and Lists,	67, 139
Kellogg, Leverett,	Hist. Goshen,	120, 154
Kellogg, Samuel,	Hist. Goshen,	118, 120
	Rolls and Lists,	22, 39
	Lists and Returns,	204
Kettle, Jonathan,	Hist. Goshen,	143, 154
	Rolls and Lists,	202
Knapp, Timothy,	Hist. Goshen,	118
	Rec. Conn. Men,	63, 223, 394, 396
	Lists and Returns,	33, 69, 170, 235
Lair, Jacob, (Layre)	Hist. Goshen,	154
	Rec. Conn. Men,	223
	Lists and Returns,	34, 69, 235
Landon, David,	Hist. Goshen,	136
	Rec. Conn. Men,	612
Langly, David,	Lists and Returns,	69

Litchfield County Revolutionary Soldiers

Name	Authority	Page
Leach, Ephraim, Jr.,	D. A. R. Lin. Book Vol. XXVIII., Enlisted at Goshen.	6
Lewis, Ebenezer,	Hist. Goshen,	154
	Rec. Conn. Men,	63, 83
	Lists and Returns,	69
	D. A. R. Lin. Book Vol. XXIII.,	59
Lewis, Nehemiah,	Hist. Goshen,	143, 154
	Rolls and Lists,	227
Lockwood, Matthew,	Hist. Goshen,	129, 142, 154
Lockwood, Seth,	Hist. Goshen,	126
	Rolls and Lists,	202
Lucas, Thomas,	Hist. Goshen,	129
	Rec. Conn. Men,	421
Lyman, Moses, Col.,	D. A. R. Lin. Book Vol. III.,	209
Mahn, Jonathan,	Hist. Goshen,	154
	Rec. Conn. Men,	93
Maltbee, Noah,	Hist. Goshen,	154
	Rec. Conn. Men,	562
Matthews, J. Hollister,	Hist. Goshen,	124, 154
	Hist. of Conn. Vol. II.,	295
Mayo, Elisha,	Hist. Goshen,	142
	Rec. Conn. Men,	228
	Goshen Statistics,	550
	Lists and Returns,	209
Merrill, Aaron,	Hist. Goshen,	155
	Rec. Conn. Men,	325, 365, 369, 635
	Lists and Returns,	274
Merrill, Ephraim,	Hist. Goshen,	155
	Rec. Conn. Men,	536
	Goshen Statistics,	550
Merrill, Jeptha,	Hist. Goshen,	128, 154
	Rec. Conn. Men,	653
	Goshen Statistics,	550
Merrill, Noah,	Hist. Goshen,	128, 138, 142
	Rec. Conn. Men,	335
	Rolls and Lists,	124
Miles, Caleb,	Hist. Goshen,	138
	Rec. Conn. Men,	224, 645
	Goshen Statistics,	499
	Lists and Returns,	69
Miles, Charles,	Rolls and Lists,	22
Miles, Daniel,	Hist. Goshen,	136
	Rec. Conn. Men,	176, 531, 612
Miles, Isaac, Sergt.,	Hist. Goshen,	118
	Rec. Conn. Men,	63, 224
	Rolls and Lists,	23
	Lists and Returns,	35, 69, 235
Mix, Elisha,	Hist. Goshen,	153
	Rec. Conn. Men,	200, 224, 320, 362, 541, 643
	Rolls and Lists,	37
	Lists and Returns,	69

Goshen

Name	Authority	Page
Mix, Stephen,	Hist. Goshen,	116
	Rec. Conn. Men,	286
	Goshen Statistics,	583, 318
	Lists and Returns,	50, 69, 172
Morris, Robert,	Hist. Goshen,	136, 138, 153
	Rec. Conn. Men,	199, 285, 612
	Lists and Returns,	69
Morse, Solomon,	Hist. Goshen,	128, 155
	Rolls and Lists,	139
Moss, Linus,	Lists and Returns,	69
Mott, Lent,	Hist. Goshen,	118, 155
Munson, Caleb,	Lists and Returns,	275
Munson, John,	Hist. Goshen,	118, 120
	Rolls and Lists,	37
Munson, Seth,	Lists and Returns,	275
Munson, Thomas E.,	Hist. Goshen,	155, 120
	Rec. Conn. Men,	635
	Rolls and Lists,	37
Nash, Martin,	Hist. Goshen,	127
	Rec. Conn. Men,	397
Negro, Jack,	Lists and Returns,	69
Negro, York, (deceased)	Lists and Returns,	50
Newell, Nathaniel,	Hist. Goshen,	155, 127
	Rec. Conn. Men,	496
North, John, Jr.,	Hist. Goshen,	119, 505
North, Seth,	Hist. Goshen,	120, 127
	Rec. Conn. Men,	512, 635
	Rolls and Lists,	39
North, Stephen,	Hist. Goshen,	127, 136
	Rec. Conn. Men,	612
	Rolls and Lists,	39
Norton, Aaron,	Hist. Goshen,	152
	Rec. Conn. Men,	77, 481, 501
Norton, Alexander,	Hist. Goshen,	155
Norton, Ebenezer,	Rec. Conn. Men,	438
Norton, Ebenezer, Jr.,	Hist. Goshen,	136, 155
	Rec. Conn. Men,	612
Norton, Eber,	Hist. Goshen,	136, 155
	Rec. Conn. Men,	612
	Rolls and Lists,	202
Norton, Jabez,	Hist. Goshen,	514
Norton, John,	Hist. Goshen,	127
	Rolls and Lists,	192
	Goshen Statistics,	1,003
	Lists and Returns,	209
	D. A. R. Lin. Book Vol. XXVIII.,	358
(Several in the service).		
Norton, Joseph,	Hist. Goshen,	127, 155
	Rolls and Lists,	68
	Rec. Conn. Men,	200, 639
	Lists and Returns,	36, 69, 172, 235

Name	Authority	Page
Norton, Levi,	Hist. Goshen, Rec. Conn. Men, Rolls and Lists,	514 549, 635 139
Norton, Medad,	Hist. Goshen, Rec. Conn. Men,	128, 136 612, 476
Norton, Miles,	Hist. Goshen, Rec. Conn. Men,	152 586
Norton, Nathan,	Hist. Goshen, Rolls and Lists,	155 37
Norton, Nathaniel,	Hist. Goshen, Rolls and Lists,	155 92, 549
Norton, Seth,	Hist. Goshen, Rec. Conn. Men,	155 123, 583
Oviatt, Benjamin,	Hist. Goshen, Rec. Conn. Men,	136 612
Parmlee, N. Stanley,	Hist. Goshen, Rec. Conn. Men,	155 536
Parmlee, Theodore,	Hist. Goshen, Rec. Conn. Men,	153 444
Peck, Elisha,	Hist. Goshen, Rec. Conn. Men, Lists and Returns,	155 365 274
Peck, Stephen,	Hist. Goshen, Rec. Conn. Men, Rolls and Lists,	155 539 194
Peck, Zebulon,	Rec. Conn. Men, Rolls and Lists, Lists and Returns,	200 90 37, 69, 236
Pickett, Daniel, (Piquet)	Hist. Goshen, Rec. Conn. Men, Lists and Returns,	155 228 209
Potter, Thaddeus,	Hist. Goshen, Rec. Conn. Men, Lists and Returns,	155 228 209
Pratt, Isaac,	Goshen Statistics, Rec. Conn. Men, D. A. R. Lin. Book Vol. XXV.,	705 166, 539 89
Price, Paul,	Hist. Goshen, Lists and Returns,	521 54
(Resided in Goshen but enlisted in Litchfield).		
Richards, Charles,	Hist. Goshen, Rec. Conn. Men,	155 562
Richards, Peter,	Hist. Goshen, Rec. Conn. Men,	155 636
Richmond, Samuel,	Hist. Goshen, Rolls and Lists,	120 37
Riley, John,	Hist. Goshen, Rolls and Lists,	120, 153 39
Rood, Robert,	Hist. Goshen, Rolls and Lists, Rec. Conn. Men,	126, 143 202 397

GOSHEN

Name	Authority	Page
Roys, Jesse, (Royce)	Hist. Goshen, Rec. Conn. Men, Rolls and Lists, Lists and Returns,	155 365 275 274
Roys, Josiah,	Hist. Goshen, Rec. Conn. Men,	136 612
Scott, ———,	Hist. Goshen,	142
Seeley, John,	Hist. Goshen, Rec. Conn. Men, Lists and Returns,	127, 138 40, 63, 195, 201, 637 40, 69, 236
Shepard, Ebenezer,	Hist. Goshen, Rec. Conn. Men, Rolls and Lists,	118, 155 62, 63, 471 21
Sherman, Rev. Josiah,	Hist. Goshen,	153
Sill, Dr. Elisha,	Hist. Goshen, Rec. Conn. Men,	143, 153 512, 631
Sill, Martin,	Rec. Conn. Men,	570
Sill, Richard,	Hist. Goshen,	155
Sizer, Nathaniel,	Lists and Returns,	69
Smith, Abraham,	Hist. Goshen, Rec. Conn. Men,	155 502, 541, 653
Smith, Asher,	Hist. Goshen, Rolls and Lists,	120, 155 37
Smith, Chileab,	Hist. Goshen, Rec. Conn. Men,	136 612, 513, 631
Smith, Israel,	Hist. Goshen, Rec. Conn. Men, Rolls and Lists,	155 365 203
Smith, Matthew,	Hist. Goshen, Rec. Conn. Men, Rolls and Lists,	138, 153 502, 548, 569 120
Squire, Charles,	Hist. Goshen, Rec. Conn. Men,	155 329
Squire, Justus,	Hist. Goshen, Rec. Conn. Men, Rolls and Lists, Lists and Returns,	120 225 39 69
Stanley, Jesse,	Hist. Goshen,	155
Stanley, Timothy, Jr.,	Hist. Goshen, Rec. Conn. Men,	127, 136 63, 612
Starr, William, Lieut.,	Hist. Goshen, Rec. Conn. Men, Rolls and Lists, Lists and Returns,	118, 126, 153 218 49, 271 69
Tankard, George,	Lists and Returns,	69
Thomson, Elisha,	Hist. Goshen, Rec. Conn. Men,	136 612
Thomson, James,	Hist. Goshen, Rolls and Lists,	153 20
Thomson, John,	Hist. Goshen, Rolls and Lists, Rec. Conn. Men,	120 139 238, 549

Name	Authority	Page
Thomson, Joseph,	Hist. Goshen,	156
	Rec. Conn. Men,	583, 644
	Rolls and Lists,	17
Thomson, Levi,	Hist. Goshen,	136
	Rec. Conn. Men,	612
Thomson, Solomon,	Hist. Goshen,	156
Thomson, Stephen,	Rec. Conn. Men,	238, 644
	Rolls and Lists,	203
Towner, Elijah,	Hist. Goshen,	126, 154
	Rec. Conn. Men,	203
	Lists and Returns,	206
Tuttle, Ichabod,	Hist. Goshen,	118, 154
	Rec. Conn. Men,	63
	Rolls and Lists,	39
	D. A. R. Lin. Book Vol. XXVIII.,	58
Tuttle, Jonathan,	Hist. Goshen,	152
	Rec. Conn. Men,	409
Tuttle, Stephen,	Hist. Goshen,	136
	Rec. Conn. Men,	612, 552
Tuttle, Timothy,	Hist. Goshen,	127, 156
Wadhams, Abraham,	Hist. Goshen,	128, 156
Wadhams, Solomon,	Lists and Returns,	274
Walter, John,	Hist. Goshen,	120, 156
	Rec. Conn. Men,	82, 226, 573, 664
	Rolls and Lists,	39
	Goshen Statistics,	788
Wheadon, Jonathan, (Wheaton)	Hist. Goshen,	118, 154
	Rolls and Lists,	39
	Lists and Returns,	69
White, John,	Lists and Returns,	69
Wicar, Thomas,	Rec. Conn. Men,	361, 369
Wilcocks, Moses,	Lists and Returns,	210
Wilcox, Elijah,	Hist. Goshen,	136, 154
	Rec. Conn. Men,	612
Willcox, Job,	Rolls and Returns,	274
Williams, Jacob,	Hist. Goshen,	118, 154
	Rec. Conn. Men,	397
	Rolls and Lists,	39, 271
Williams, Jacob, Jr.,	Hist. Goshen,	118, 156
	Rec. Conn. Men,	63
Willoughby, John, (deserted)	Lists and Returns,	50, 69
Willson, Jobe,	Rec. Conn. Men,	363
Wire, Thomas,	Hist. Goshen,	118, 138
	Rec. Conn. Men,	63
	Rolls and Lists,	39, 91
	Lists and Returns,	177, 271
Wright, Charles,	Rec. Conn. Men,	63
Wright, David,	Hist. Goshen,	118, 154
	Rec. Conn. Men,	62, 63
	Rolls and Lists,	21

GOSHEN

Name	Authority	Page
Wright, Freedom,	Hist. Goshen,	570
	Rec. Conn. Men,	63
Wright, Jabez, Capt.,	Rec. Conn. Men,	548
	Rolls and Lists,	209, 210, 225
Wright, John, Capt.,	Rolls and Lists,	58, 61, 97, 230
Wyard, Thomas,	Lists and Returns,	44, 69, 236

Harwinton

Revolutionary Soldiers

OF

Harwinton

COMPILED BY
MARY FLOYD TALLMADGE CHAPTER
DAUGHTERS OF THE AMERICAN REVOLUTION
LITCHFIELD, CONN.

For fuller accounts of these men see original lists

Revolutionary Soldiers of Harwinton

Name	Authority	Page
Agard, Salmon, Sergt.,		
Alfred, Job,	Dwight C. Kilbourn.	
	Rec. Conn. Men,	232
Andrus, David,	Gen. Huntington's Note Book.	
Austin, Eusebius, Sergt.,	Rec. Conn. Men,	583
Baldwin, Erastus,	Rec. Conn. Men,	663
Barber, Benjamin,	Hist. Harwinton,	115
	Lists and Returns,	6
Barber, Joseph,	Rec. Conn. Men,	562
Barber, Reuben,	D. A. R. Lin. Book Vol. XV.,	266
Barber, Simeon,	Hist. Harwinton,	115
	Rec. Conn. Men,	663
Barber, Timothy,	Hist. Harwinton,	115
	Lists and Returns,	6
Barnes, Nathan,	Hist. Harwinton,	115
Bartholomew, Benjamin,	Rec. Conn. Men,	562
Bradley, Joseph,	Rolls and Lists,	67
Bull, Gurden,	Rec. Conn. Men,	583
Butler, David,	Lists and Returns,	280
Butler, Isaiah, Jr.,	Hist. Harwinton,	115
	Lists and Returns,	6
Butler, Solomon,	Hist. Harwinton,	115
	Lists and Returns,	6
Butler, Stephen,	D. A. R. Lin. Book Vol. XXI.,	47
Catlin, Abijah,	Year Book S. A. R. 1897-99,	315
	D. A. R. Lin. Book Vol. XIV.,	344
Catlin, Abraham,	Hist. Harwinton,	115
	Lists and Returns,	6
Catlin Eli, Lieut.,	Hist. Harwinton,	115
	Lists and Returns,	6
Catlin, George,	D. A. R. Lin. Book Vol. XIX.,	121
Catlin, Hezekiah,	App. for Pension.	
	Lists and Returns,	278
Catlin, Jacob,	Year Book S. A. R. 1897-99,	315
Catlin, Lewis	Litchfield Scrap Book,	4
Catlin, Phineas,	Hist. Harwinton,	115
Catlin, Roswell,	Hist. Harwinton,	115
	Lists and Returns,	71
Clark, Lyman,	Hist. Harwinton,	114
	Rec. Conn. Men,	663
	See Litchfield List.	
Cook, Daniel,	Hist. Harwinton,	115
	Lists and Returns,	6

Name	Authority	Page
Cook, Jonathan,	Hist. Harwinton,	115
	Lists and Returns,	6
Cook, Joseph,	D. A. R. Lin. Book Vol. XVII.,	12
Cook, Oliver,	Hist. Camden, N. Y.,	533
Cook, Ozem,	Hist. Harwinton,	115
	Lists and Returns,	71
Cook, Samuel, Jr.,	Rec. Conn. Men,	562
Elmore, Caleb,	Hist. Harwinton,	115
(Elmer)	Lists and Returns,	28
Ely, Jacob, Sergt.,	D. A. R. Lin. Book Vol. XI.,	124
Foot, Beriah,	Hist. Harwinton,	115
Foot, Darius,	Hist. Harwinton,	114
	Rec. Conn. Men,	663
Foot, Ebenezer,	Lists and Returns,	28, 236
Frisbie, Jabez,	Rolls and Lists,	79
	Lists and Returns,	6
Frisbie, John,	Rec. Conn. Men,	562
Gilbert, Amus,	Lists and Returns,	6
Greene, Thomas,	Hist. Harwinton,	115
	Lists and Returns,	71, 203
Gridley, Seth,	Hist. Harwinton,	115
	Lists and Returns,	30, 168
Gridley, Silas,	Hist. Harwinton,	115
Griswold, Asa,	Hist. Harwinton,	115
	Lists and Returns,	6
Griswold, White,	Hist. Harwinton,	115
	Lists and Returns,	6
Halstead, Joseph,	Hist. Harwinton,	115
	Lists and Returns,	71
Halstead, Timothy,	Lists and Returns,	285
Hawley, Joseph C.,	Hist. Harwinton,	115
	Rolls and Lists,	18
	Lists and Returns,	6, 71
Haydon, Allyn,	Hist. Harwinton,	115
	Lists and Returns,	6
Hinsdale, Elisha,	Hist. Harwinton,	115
	Lists and Returns,	71
Hinsdale, Ezra,	D. A. R. Lin. Book Vol. XI.,	236
Hinsdale, Jacob,	D. A. R. Lin. Book Vol. XVIII.,	184
Hinsdale, Samuel,	Hist. Harwinton,	115
	Lists and Returns,	71
Hodge, Asahel, Lieut.,	Hist. Harwinton,	115
Capt.-Adj.,	Rolls and Lists,	75
	Rec Conn. Men,	229, 346, 374
	Lists and Returns,	31, 71
Holt, Livenus,	Rolls and Lists,	62
	Lists and Returns,	6
Hopkins, Hezekiah,	D. A. R. Lin. Book Vol. XXII.,	91
Hopkins, Nehemiah,	D. A. R. Lin. Book Vol. XX.,	213
Johnson, Benoni,	Hist. Harwinton	115
	Rec. Conn. Men,	663

HARWINTON

Name	Authority	Page
Johnson, Hamlin,	Rolls and Lists,	67
Jones, George,	Hist. Harwinton,	115
	Rec. Conn. Men,	663
	Lists and Returns,	6
Jones, James,	Lists and Returns,	286
	Rec. Conn. Men,	283
Johnson, Christopher,	Hist. Harwinton,	115
	Lists and Returns,	6
Johnson, Samuel,	Hist. Harwinton,	115
	Lists and Returns,	6
Kellogg, Allen,	Rec. Conn. Men,	583
Lambert, Samuel,	Hist. Harwinton,	115
	Rolls and Lists,	55
	Lists and Returns,	6
Leach, Hezekiah,	Hist. Harwinton,	115
	Lists and Returns,	6, 266
Loomis, Elijah,	Hist. Harwinton,	115
	Lists and Returns,	6
	Rec. Conn. Men,	279
Loomis George,	Hist. Harwinton,	115
	Lists and Returns,	6
Maisy, Ezekiel,	Rec. Conn. Men,	573
Marshall, Elisha,	Lists and Returns,	35, 236
Merriman, George,	Rec. Conn. Men,	562
Monson, Levi, Sergt.,	Hist. Harwinton,	114
Northaway, Asa,	Rec. Conn. Men,	274
Olcutt, James, Jr.,	Hist. Harwinton,	115
	Lists and Returns,	6
Phelps, Hezekiah,	Hist. Harwinton,	115
	Lists and Returns,	6
Phelps, Ira,	Rec. Conn. Men,	583
Phelps, Oliver,	Hist. Harwinton,	115
	Rolls and Lists,	20
	Lists and Returns,	6
Phelps, Samuel, Jr.,	Hist. Harwinton,	115
	Lists and Returns,	6
Porter, Ashbel,	Hist. Harwinton,	115
	Lists and Returns,	6
Potter, Jesse,	Hist. Harwinton,	115
	Lists and Returns,	6
Rathbun, John,	Rec. Conn. Men,	570
Rossiter, Timothy,	Rec. Conn. Men,	281
	Lists and Returns,	187
Scott, Elijah,	Hist. Harwinton,	115
	Lists and Returns,	40
Scott, Enos,	Hist. Harwinton,	115
	Rolls and Lists,	20
	Lists and Returns,	6, 71
Scott, Ethiel, (Ithiel)	Hist. Harwinton,	115
	Rolls and Lists,	76, 104
	Lists and Returns,	71

LITCHFIELD COUNTY REVOLUTIONARY SOLDIERS

Name	Authority	Page
Skinner, Ashbel,	Rec. Conn. Men,	583
Skinner, Zimri,	Hist. Harwinton,	115
	Lists and Returns,	6
Smith, Jesse,	Gen. Huntington's Note Book.	
Stedman, Timothy,	Hist. Harwinton,	115
	Lists and Returns,	71
Walsore, Moses,	Rolls and Lists,	55
Wesson, Samuel,	Hist. Harwinton,	115
	Lists and Returns,	6
Wesson, Samuel, Jr.,	Lists and Returns,	6
White, Nathaniel,	Rec. Conn. Men,	562
Wilcox, James,	Hist. Harwinton,	115
	Lists and Returns,	43, 71
Wilson, Abner,	Hist. Harwinton,	115
	Lists and Returns,	6
Wilson, John,	Hist. of Camden, N. Y.,	197, 535
Winchell, John,	Hist. Harwinton,	115
	Rec. Conn. Men,	663

Kent

Revolutionary Soldiers

OF

Kent

COMPILED BY
ROGER SHERMAN CHAPTER
DAUGHTERS OF THE AMERICAN REVOLUTION
NEW MILFORD, CONN.

Revolutionary Soldiers of Kent

Name	Authority	Page
Ashly, John,	Lists and Returns,	103
Avery, Daniel,	Rec. Conn. Men,	220
Baltier, George,	App. for Pension.	
Barlow, John,	Rec. Conn. Men,	220
	Lists and Returns,	23, 107, 235
Barnum, Amos, Sergt.,	Rec. Conn. Men,	364
	App. for Pension.	
	Lists and Returns,	23, 104, 165, 235
Barnum, Sam'l., Lieut.,	Lists and Returns,	23, 165, 235
Barnum, Stephen, Sergt.,	Rec. Conn. Men,	218
	Lists and Returns,	23, 103, 165, 235
Barnum, Zenas,	Lists and Returns,	104
Barlee, Michael,	App. for Pension.	
	With Paul Jones.	
Bates, Samuel,	Rec. Conn. Men,	361, 220
	Lists and Returns,	103
Batterson, George,	Rec. Conn. Men,	69, 366, 632
	Stiles Ancient Windsor Vol. II.,	68
Beaumont, Lemuel,	Rec. Conn. Men,	366
Beaumont, Matthew,	Rec. Conn. Men,	361
Becher, Jonathan,	App. for Pension.	
Beeman, Daniel,	Rec. Conn. Men,	120
Beeman, Elisha,	Lists and Returns,	106
Beeman, Ezekiel,	Rec. Conn. Men,	574
	Lists and Returns,	189
Beeman, Lemuel,	App. for Pension.	
	Lists and Returns,	106
Beeman, Tracy,	Rec. Conn. Men,	664
Beeman, Truman,	Lists and Returns,	210
Beemand, Lemuel,	Rec. Conn. Men,	220
Beemand, Matthias, Corp.,	Rec. Conn. Men,	220
Beeny, John,	Lists and Returns,	106
Berry, Barnabas,	Rec. Conn. Men,	539
Berry, John,	Rec. Conn. Men,	539
Berry, Kellogg,	Rec. Conn. Men,	652, 662
Berry, Lemuel,	Rec. Conn. Men,	652
Bolt, Benjamin,	Lists and Returns,	103
Bradshaw, William,	Lists and Returns,	103
Brown, John,	Rec. Conn. Men,	220
	Lists and Returns,	106
Buckley, Calvin,	Rec. Conn. Men,	362
Burton, John,	Rec. Conn. Men,	220

Name	Authority	Page
Carter, Heman,	Rec. Conn. Men,	366
Carter, Joseph,	Rec. Conn. Men,	221
Carter, Samuel,	Rec. Conn. Men,	221
Chamberlain, Leander,	Rec. Conn. Men,	361
Chamberlain, Peleg,	Rec. Conn. Men,	466
Chamberlain, Samuel,	Rec. Conn. Men,	221
	Lists and Returns,	104
Chamberlain, Swift,	Rec. Conn. Men,	366
	Lists and Returns,	285
Chapman, Elijah,	Rec. Conn. Men,	221
	Lists and Returns,	103
Cheney, Richard,	Lists and Returns,	25, 235, 355, 165
Clark, Cyreno,	App. for Pension.	
Cobb, John,	Rec. Conn. Men,	221
Coggswell, Edward,	Hist. New Milford,	229
Comstalk, Cuff,	Lists and Returns,	103
Curtice, George,	Lists and Returns,	26, 106, 165, 235
Curtiss, Eleazer, Jr., Capt.,	Rec. Conn. Men,	61
Curtiss, Eleazer, Major,	Rec. Conn. Men,	537
Danes, David,	Rec. Conn. Men,	222
	Lists and Returns,	107
Deland, Aaron,	App. for Pension.	
Devine, Timothy,	Hist. New Milford,	229
Dickison, Joseph,	Rec. Conn. Men,	222
Die, Daniell, (Dye)	Lists and Returns,	27, 104
Dixon, Joseph,	Lists and Returns,	104
Dodge, Stephen, Lieut.,	Rec. Conn. Men,	586, 614
Downs, Patrick,	Lists and Returns,	106
Drew, Peter,	Rec. Conn. Men,	569
Eaton, Moses,	Rec. Conn. Men,	69, 415
Fairchild, Ezra,	Rec. Conn. Men,	583
Fairchild, Samuel,	Rec. Conn. Men,	222
	Lists and Returns,	104
Fenn, Thomas,	Lists and Returns,	106
Finney, John,	Lists and Returns,	106
Fisher, Henry,	Hist. New Milford,	229
Fitch, ———, Corp.,	Rec. Conn. Men,	361
Fitch, James,	Lists and Returns,	209
Fitch, Prentiss,	Rec. Conn. Men,	222
	Lists and Returns,	104
Folker, Ebenezer, (Forker)	Rec. Conn. Men,	634
	App. for Pension.	
	Lists and Returns,	106
Forgues, Ebenezer,	Rec. Conn. Men,	361, 369
Freeman, Coll,	Rec. Conn. Men,	222
Freeman, Cuff,	Rec. Conn. Men,	222
	Lists and Returns,	103
Fuller, Abraham, Capt.,	Rec. Conn. Men,	466
	D. A. R. Lin. Book Vol. XXVII.,	253

KENT

Name	Authority	Page
Fuller, Asabel, Fifer,	Rec. Conn. Men,	466
Fuller, Oliver, Capt.,	Hist. New Milford,	704
Gear, Alpheus,	Rec. Conn. Men,	329
Gear, Nathaniel,	Rec. Conn. Men,	466
	Lists and Returns,	208
Goodyear, Edward,	Lists and Returns,	107
Graham, John,	Lists and Returns,	106
Gray, Elijah,	Rec. Conn. Men,	583
	D. A. R. Lin. Book Vol. XXIV.,	270
Hatch, Jethro,	Rec. Conn. Men,	503
	Born in Tolland.	
	D. A. R. Lin. Book Vol. XXV.,	175
Hawes, Samuel,	Lists and Returns,	106
Hills, Ebenezer, Capt.,	Rec. Conn. Men,	296
	Lists and Returns,	31, 106, 169, 235
Holmes, Peleg,	Lists and Returns,	106
Holloway, John,	App. for Pension.	
Hubbell, David,	App. for Pension.	
Hubbell, Primus,	Lists and Returns,	103
Hubbell, Samuel,	Lists and Returns,	104
Ingraham, Henry,	Lists and Returns,	208
Ingraham, Samuel,	Rec. Conn. Men,	362
	Lists and Returns,	282
Judd, ———,	App. for Pension.	
Lake, Rogers,	Rec. Conn. Men,	366
	Lists and Returns,	282
Lake, William,	Rec. Conn. Men,	363
Lamkin, Benjamin,	Rec. Conn. Men,	224
(Lamskin)	Lists and Returns,	34, 170, 235
Leonard, Silas,	App. for Pension.	
Loff, David,	Rec. Conn. Men,	259
Main, John,	Rolls and Lists,	90
	Lists and Returns,	104, 235
Mallery, Nathan,	Lists and Returns,	282
Merwin, Jesse,	Lists and Returns,	104
More, John, Jr.,	Lists and Returns,	35
Morey, Stephen,	Rec. Conn. Men,	363
Murray, Joel,	Lists and Returns,	106
Murray, Noah, Sergt.,	Rolls and Lists,	89
	Lists and Returns,	35, 106, 235
Palmer, Amos,	Rec. Conn. Men,	229
Peck, Ebenezer,	App. for Pension.	
Peck, Reuben,	Rec. Conn. Men,	583
Pennell, Isaac, Sergt.,	Rec. Conn. Men,	258
Phinney, ———, Sergt.,	Rec. Conn. Men,	361
Raymond, Newcomb,	Rec. Conn. Men,	366
	D. A. R. Lin. Book Vol. XXIV.,	271
Reilly, John,	App. for Pension.	
Richards, Sam.,	Lists and Returns,	107

Litchfield County Revolutionary Soldiers

Name	Authority	Page
Roberts, Asiah,	Lists and Returns,	107
Root, Daniel,	App. for Pension.	
Rowley, Seth,	Rec. Conn. Men,	259
Segar, Joseph,	Rec. Conn. Men, Pensioner.	664
Simpson, Elipt.,	Lists and Returns,	104
*Skeel, Jonathan,	D. A. R. Lin. Book Vol. XXIII., Vol. XXV.,	99, 163
Slade, John,	App. for Pension.	
Sperry, Dorias,	Lists and Returns,	104
Sprague, Asa,	Rec. Conn. Men, Lists and Returns,	362, 106
Sprague, James,	Gen. Huntington's Note Book.	
Smith, John,	Lists and Returns,	103
Smith, Noah,	Rec. Conn. Men, Lists and Returns,	228, 484, 557, 208
Starkweather, Asa,	Lists and Returns,	107
Stone, Daniel,	Rec. Conn. Men, Pensioner.	664
Stone, David,	App. for Pension.	
Stone, Levi,	Rec. Conn. Men,	68, 658
Sucknuck, Daniel,	Lists and Returns,	103
Sweetland, Daniel,	Rec. Conn. Men,	364
Swift, Jeirah, Capt.,	Rec. Conn. Men,	110
Swift, Nathaniel,	App. for Pension.	
Swift, Philetus,	Rec. Conn. Men, Lists and Returns,	366, 282
Tanner, Ebenezer, (Cincinnati Soc.	Rec. Conn. Men, Enlisted in Kent and Cornwall).	375
Talker, Ebenezer,	Lists and Returns,	285
Tayler, James,	Gen. Huntington's Note Book.	
Taylor, Elias,	App. for Pension.	
Temple, Frederick,	Lists and Returns,	106
Thayer, David,	Rec. Conn. Men,	261
Thomas, John,	Lists and Returns,	106
Thompson, Comfort,	Rec. Conn. Men,	329
Warren, John,	Rec. Conn. Men, Lists and Returns,	226, 106
Warrups, Thomas,	Lists and Returns,	103
Warwehen, Peter,	Lists and Returns,	103
Waters, Elihu,	Rec. Conn. Men,	251
Wedge, Stephen,	App. for Pension.	
Welch, John,	App. for Pension.	
Welsh, Michael,	Lists and Returns,	107
Wheeler, Nathan,	Rec. Conn. Men, Lists and Returns,	361, 106, 282
Whitehead, David,	Pensioner. Sup. Court Records Vol. XVI., Rec. Conn. Men,	4, 664

Name	Authority	Page
Whitlock, Joel,	Lists and Returns,	106
Wilkinson, Thomas,	App. for Pension.	
Woodward, Thomas,	Lists and Returns,	107
Woolman, Miles,	Gen. Huntington's Note Book.	
Wines, Peter,	Lists and Returns,	211

Also, the Scatacook Tribe of Indians furnished 100 warriors for the Revolutionary War.—Hist. of Connecticut by John Barber, Published 1836.

New Hartford

Revolutionary Soldiers

OF

New Hartford

COMPILED BY
MARY FLOYD TALLMADGE CHAPTER
DAUGHTERS OF THE AMERICAN REVOLUTION
LITCHFIELD, CONN.

Revolutionary Soldiers of New Hartford

Name	Authority	Page
Adams, Benjamin, Sergt.,	Rec. Conn. Men,	17, 49, 526, 540
Andrews, Eli,	Rec. Conn. Men,	17
Andrews, James,	Rec. Conn. Men,	158
Andrus, Ezra,	Lists and Returns,	21, 55, 163, 252
Andrus, Theodore,	Lists and Returns,	250
Arnold, Jonathan,	Lists and Returns,	240
Austin, Aaron,	Lin. Book No. 10,	291
	Lin. Book No. 12,	131
	Lin. Book No. 19,	79
	Rec. Conn. Men,	17, 110, 441, 492, 632, 648
Austin, James, Ensign,	Rec. Conn. Men,	17, 540
(Perhaps belonged to Barkhamsted).		
Barnes, Stephen,	Lin. Book No. 17,	323
	Rec. Conn. Men,	17, 282
	Lists and Returns,	261, 282
Barnes, Timothy, Jr.,	Rec. Conn. Men,	17
Bass, Nathan, Sergt.,	Rec. Conn. Men,	17, 471
Bates, Phineas,	Rec. Conn. Men,	17
Benham, Elias,	Rec. Conn. Men,	17
See Barkhamsted List.		
Benham, James,	Lists and Returns,	287
Benham, Jehiel,	Rec. Conn. Men,	17, 40
Bennett, Jabin,	Lists and Returns,	256
Bidwell, Thomas, Ensign,	Rec. Conn. Men,	17, 86, 228, 633, 666
	Lin. Book No. 20,	239
Bonnum, James,	Lists and Returns,	207
Burnham, Reuben, Sergt.,	Rec. Conn. Men,	17
Cadwell, Phineas,	Lists and Returns,	252
Case, Abraham, Jr.,	Rec. Conn. Men,	17, 49
Case, Elijah, Sergt.,	Rec. Conn. Men,	17, 196
See Barkhamsted List.		
Case, William, 2nd.,	Rec. Conn. Men,	17, 50
Case, Zacheus, Capt.,	Rec. Conn. Men,	17, 474, 499, 624
Chapin, David,	Lists and Returns,	250
Chapin, Phineas,	Lists and Returns,	243
Chubbs, Stephen, Corp.,	Rec. Conn. Men,	17, 444, 483
Collins, Nathaniel, Sergt.,	Rec. Conn. Men,	7, 17, 291, 471, 651
Cook, Jabez,	Lists and Returns,	282
Coville, David,	Rec. Conn. Men,	17, 642
Crane, Ebenezer,	Rec. Conn. Men,	17, 551
See Barkhamsted List.		
Crosby, Obed,	Rec. Conn. Men,	17, 61, 219, 471

Name	Authority	Page
Crown, Shubael,	Lists and Returns,	278
Dyer, Daniel, Sergt.,	Rec. Conn. Men,	17, 499
Edgecomb, Ezra,	Lists and Returns,	28, 56
Elwell, Joshua, Corp.,	Rec. Conn. Men, See Barkhamsted List.	17, 471
Ensign, Elias,	Rec. Conn. Men,	17
Ensign, Eliphalet,	Rec. Conn. Men,	17, 483
Ensign, Otis,	Lin. Book No. 21,	22
Fay, John,	Lists and Returns,	250
Fay, Timothy,	Lists and Returns,	258
Fisher, Daniel,	Rec. Conn. Men,	17
Fox, Bassett,	Lists and Returns,	276
Fox, Simeon,	Lists and Returns,	264, 276
Flower, Zephon,	Lists and Returns,	280
Flowers, Elijah,	Lists and Returns,	29, 55, 167
Flowers, Elisha,	Lists and Returns,	242
Flowers, Gabriel, Tr'm't'r.,	Rec. Conn. Men,	17, 83, 483
Fuller, Isaac, Jr.,	Rec. Conn. Men,	17
Garrit, John,	Lists and Returns,	56
Gayland, Josiah,	Lists and Returns,	243
Gilbert, Asa,	Rec. Conn. Men, Lin. Book No. 16,	17, 274, 473, 634, 653 22
(Two Asa Gilberts in the service).		
Gilbert, John,	Rec. Conn. Men, Lin. Book No. 5, Lin. Book No. 9, Lin. Book No. 10, Lin. Book, No. 11, Lin. Book No. 18,	17, 79, 117, 204, 623 256 135 199 41 229
Gilbert, Joseph,	Rec. Conn. Men, Lin. Book No. 25, Lists and Returns,	17, 113, 219, 532, 642 285 55, 168, 252
Gilbert, Theodore,	Lists and Returns,	55, 168, 250
Gillet, Adna,	Lists and Returns,	168, 355
Goss, Thomas,	Rec. Conn. Men, See Barkhamsted List.	17, 471
Griswold, Francis,	Rec. Conn. Men,	17, 227
Hale, Reuben,	Rec. Conn. Men, Lists and Returns,	223, 364, 643 71
Hall, Levi,	Rec. Conn. Men,	17, 62, 654
Hill, David, Jr.,	Rec. Conn. Men,	17
Hinman, Asher, Sergt.,	Rec. Conn. Men,	17
Hopkins, George,	Lists and Returns,	249
Hopkins, Roderick,	Rec. Conn. Men, Lists and Returns,	17, 247, 642 245
Humphrey, Charles,	Rec. Conn. Men,	17, 495
Humphrey, George,	Rec. Conn. Men, Lin. Book No. 3,	17, 49, 474 258
Humphrey, Oliver, Jr.,	Rec. Conn. Men, Lin. Book No. 3,	17, 49 258

New Hartford

Name	Authority	Page
Humphrey, Solomon, Jr.,	Rec. Conn. Men,	17
	Lin. Book No. 11,	339
	Lin. Book No. 13,	140
Humphrey, Theophilus,	Rec. Conn. Men,	17, 49
	Lin. Book No. 11,	176
Hurlburt, Josiah,	Rec. Conn. Men,	17
Ives, John,	Rec. Conn. Men,	17, 199, 329, 471, 643
	Lin. Book No. 5,	217
	See Barkhamsted List.	
Kellogg, Leverett,	Rec. Conn. Men,	17
Kellogg, Moses,	Rec. Conn. Men,	17
King, Jonathan,	Rec. Conn. Men,	17, 412, 531, 540
	See Barkhamsted List.	
Marsh, Daniel, Sergt.,	Rec. Conn. Men,	13, 17, 424
Marsh, John,	Rec. Conn. Men,	345
	See Barkhamsted List.	
Merrell, Aaron,	Lists and Returns,	56
Merrell, Cyprian, (Merrills)	Rec. Conn. Men,	17, 250
	Lists and Returns,	34, 55
Merrell, Eliakin, Jr.,	Rec. Conn. Men,	17
Merrell, Elijah,	Lin. Book No. 13,	9
Merrell, Jerijah,	Rec. Conn. Men,	17, 470
Merrell, Noah,	Lists and Returns,	287
Merrell, Solomon,	Rec. Conn. Men,	17, 483
Merrill, Phineas,	Rec. Conn. Men,	17, 83, 627, 628
	Lin. Book No. 15,	183
Mills, Amasa, Lieut.,	Rec. Conn. Men,	17, 492, 548, 635, 666
	Lin. Book No. 3,	126, 127
Mills, Benjamin, Sergt.,	Rec. Conn. Men,	17, 61, 540, 548, 616
Mills, Ephraim, Corp.,	Rec. Conn. Men,	17, 50, 474
	Lin. Book No. 18,	328
Mills, Gideon, (Canton)	Rec. Conn. Men,	17, 49, 616
Mills, Samuel,	Rec. Conn. Men,	17, 24, 272, 375, 424
	Lin. Book No. 5,	95
	Lin. Book No. 9,	10
Mix, Benjamin,	Lists and Returns,	254
Northaway, George,	Rec. Conn. Men,	17, 474
Norton, John, Ensign,	Rec. Conn. Men,	6, 17, 228, 582, 583
	Lin. Book No. 4,	274
	Lin. Book No. 7,	255
	Lin. Book, No. 8,	227
	Lin. Book No. 12,	287
	Lin. Book No. 16,	366
	Lin. Book No. 18,	100
	See Barkhamsted List.	
Olcott, Thomas, Jr.,	Rec. Conn. Men,	17
Olmsted, Garmaliel,	Lists and Returns,	250
Payne, Jesse,	Rec. Conn. Men,	17, 50
Pease, William,	Rec. Conn. Men,	17, 62
Pinney, David,	Rec. Conn. Men,	17
Pitkin, Caleb,	Rec. Conn. Men,	17

Litchfield County Revolutionary Soldiers

Name	Authority	Page
Rexford, William,	Rec. Conn. Men, See Barkhamsted List.	17
Roberts, Elisha,	Lists and Returns,	38, 55, 173, 257
Rockwell, John,	Rec. Conn. Men,	17, 61, 74, 644
Rust, Aloney,	Lin. Book No. 27,	6
Seymour, Elias,	Lists and Returns,	55
Seymour, Elijah, Corp.,	Rec. Conn. Men,	17, 444, 483, 549
Seymour, Uriah, Lieut.,	Rec. Conn. Men,	17, 483, 492
	Lin. Book No. 5,	68
	Lin. Book No. 6,	324
	Lin. Book No. 7,	236
	Lin. Book No. 13,	189
	Lin. Book No. 16,	189
Seymour, William,	Lin. Book No. 22,	81
Shepard, Ebenezer,	Rec. Conn. Men,	17, 62, 63, 471
Shepard, Joseph, Jr.,	Rec. Conn. Men,	17
	Lin. Book, No. 5,	267
	Lin. Book No. 15,	59
Shepard, Moses, Sergt.,	Rec. Conn. Men, See Barkhamsted List.	17, 60, 625
Shepard, Phenious,	Lists and Returns,	249
Simons, Joseph,	Lists and Returns,	259
Simons, William,	Rec. Conn. Men,	17, 385
Smith, Seth, Capt.,	Rec. Conn. Men,	17, 22, 24, 656
	Lin. Book No. 3,	107
	Lists and Returns,	276
Spencer, Ashbel,	Rec. Conn. Men,	17
Spencer, James,	Lists and Returns,	253
Spencer, Noah,	Lists and Returns,	208
Steaphens, Aaron, (Stevens)	Lists and Returns,	39, 55, 254
Steel, Rhoderick,	Rec. Conn. Men,	17, 417
Steel, William, Jr.,	Rec. Conn. Men,	17
Steele, Isaac,	Rec. Conn. Men,	17, 88, 473, 653
	Lin. Book No. 4,	326
Taylor, Child,	Rec. Conn. Men,	17, 61
Taylor, John,	Lists and Returns,	41, 56, 175
Taylor, Obediah,	Lists and Returns,	208, 287
Tiffany, Timothy,	Rec. Conn. Men,	17, 102, 404, 653, 660
Tyler, Amos,	Lists and Returns,	287
Wallen, Daniel,	Lists and Returns,	207
Ward, John,	Lists and Returns,	177
Watson, Levi,	Lists and Returns,	208
Watson, Zechariah,	Rec. Conn. Men,	17, 83, 424
Webb, Jonas,	Rec. Conn. Men,	17
Webster, Nathan,	Rec. Conn. Men,	17, 83, 164, 476
White, Lemuel,	Lists and Returns,	207
Wilder, Ephraim,	Rec. Conn. Men,	17, 471
	Lin. Book No. 4, See Barkhamsted List.	173

New Hartford

Name	Authority	Page
Wilder, Gamaliel,	Rec. Conn. Men, See Barkhamsted List.	17
Wilder, John,	Rec. Conn. Men,	17, 471
Willcox, Asa,	Rec. Conn. Men,	17, 50, 417, 582
Wright, Charles,	Rec. Conn. Men,	17, 548, 625, 638

New Milford

Revolutionary Soldiers

OF

New Milford

COMPILED BY
ROGER SHERMAN CHAPTER
DAUGHTERS OF THE AMERICAN REVOLUTION
NEW MILFORD, CONN.

Revolutionary Soldiers of New Milford

Name	Authority	Page
Abernethy, James,	Lists and Returns,	102
Adams, Benjamin,	Hist. New Milford,	218
Averill, Nathaniel,	Hist. New Milford,	218
Baker, Phineas,	Lists and Returns,	102
Baldwin, Isaac, Surgeon,	Hist. New Milford,	646
	Rec. Conn. Men,	628
Baldwin, Isaac,	Hist. New Milford,	224
	Rec. Conn. Men,	549
	Lineage Book Vol. XXIV.,	254
Baldwin, Israel, 2nd, Lt.,	Hist. New Milford,	641
Baldwin, Jared,	Hist. New Milford,	218
Baldwin, John,	Hist. New Milford,	218
Baldwin, Jonah,	Hist. New Milford,	643
	Rec. Conn. Men,	581
Baldwin, Simeon,	Lineage Book Vol. XXV.,	334
Baldwin, Theophilus,	Hist. New Milford,	641
	Rec. Conn. Men,	82, 221
	Lineage Book Vol. XXIV.,	132
Bardsley, Stiles,	Hist. New Milford,	218
Barnes, Caleb,	Hist. New Milford,	218
Barns, Abraham,	Lists and Returns,	55, 74, 106
Beach, David, Lieut.,	Rec. Conn. Men,	82, 194, 322, 375
	Lists and Returns,	55, 105
Beach, John,	Hist. New Milford,	218, 648
Beeman, Mathias,	Hist. New Milford,	218
Beers, James,	Lists and Returns,	105
Bennett, James, Lieut.,	Rec. Conn. Men,	218, 352, 373
	Lists and Returns,	55, 101
Bennett, Samuel, Ensign,	Hist. New Milford,	652
	Rec. Conn. Men,	279, 576
Blakeley, David,	Lists and Returns,	102
Boardman, Elijah,	Rolls and Lists,	31
Booth, Edwin,	Rec. Conn. Men,	21
	Gen. Huntington's Note Book.	
Bostwick, Amos, Ensign,	Rec. Conn. Men,	104, 105
	Hist. New Milford,	577
Bostwick, Benjamin,	Hist. New Milford,	217
Bostwick, David,	Hist. New Milford,	218
	Lists and Returns,	55, 105
Bostwick, Ebenezer, Sergt.,	Hist. New Milford,	224
	Lists and Returns,	24, 55, 73, 105, 163

Litchfield County Revolutionary Soldiers

Name	Authority	Page
Bostwick, Elisha, 2nd, Lt.,	Rec. Conn. Men,	82, 104, 105
Bostwick, Elizur,	Rec. Conn. Men,	82
Bostwick, Isaac, Capt.,	Hist. New Milford,	218
	Rec. Conn. Men,	104
Bostwick, Israel,	Hist. New Milford,	218
Bostwick, Joel,	Hist. New Milford,	218
Bostwick, Jonathan,	Rec. Conn. Men,	203, 652
Bostwick, Nathan, Ensign,	Rec. Conn. Men,	218
Bostwick, Oliver, Lieut.,	Rec. Conn. Men,	63, 218, 629
	Hist. New Milford,	224
	Lists and Returns,	55, 101
Bostwick, Reuben, Capt.,	Rec. Conn. Men,	393, 548, 614
	Hist. New Milford,	224
Bostwick, Salmon,	Hist. New Milford,	218
	Rolls and Lists,	110
	Lists and Returns,	105
Bradshaw, James,	Rec. Conn. Men,	294
Briggs, Zephania, Lieut.,	Rec. Conn. Men,	70, 650
Brownson, Benjamin, Capt.,	Rec. Conn. Men,	612
	Hist. New Milford,	220
Brownson, Mathew, Sergt.,	Hist. New Milford,	218
Brownson, Reuben,	Rec. Conn. Men,	583
Bryant, William,	Lists and Returns,	102
Buck, Daniel,	D. A. R. Lin. Book Vol. XIX.,	334
Buck, James, Capt.,	D. A. R. Lineage Book Vol. XIII.,	109
Buck, Josiah,	Rec. Conn. Men,	63, 158, 218
	Lists and Returns,	24, 101, 163
Buel, David, Corp.,	Rec. Conn. Men,	281, 632
	Hist. New Milford,	218, 846
	Lists and Returns,	24, 163
Buns, (Bunce) Isaiah, (and Washington)	Lists and Returns,	24, 55, 74, 106
Burritt, Stephen,	Rec. Conn. Men,	583
Burt, David,	Rev. Sol. Scrap Book,	42
Cain, William, Fifer,	Rolls and Lists,	110
	Lists and Returns,	26, 55, 74, 101, 106
Camp, Isaac,	Rev. Sol. Scrap Book,	42
Camp, Israel,	Hist. New Milford,	218
Camp, Jesse,	Hist. New Milford,	218
Camp, John, Corp.,	Rec. Conn. Men,	209, 280
	Hist. New Milford,	679
Canfield, Elijah,		
Canfield, Ezeriah, (Azariah)	Rec. Conn. Men,	363
	Lists and Returns,	101
Canfield, John,	Hist. New Milford,	218
	D. A. R. Lin. Book Vol. XXIV.,	66, 75
Canfield, Judson,	Rec. Conn. Men,	492
Canfield, Nathaniel,	Rec. Conn. Men,	574
Canfield, Samuel, Col.,	Rec. Conn. Men,	424, 436
	Hist. New Milford,	681
	D. A. R. Lin. Book Vol. XXV.,	181

Name	Authority	Page
Cary, Elijah,	Hist. New Milford,	218
Case, John,	Rec. Conn. Men,	583
Cavenan, John,	Rec. Conn. Men,	663
Chatfield, Levi,	Rec. Conn. Men,	209, 633
	Hist. New Milford,	261
Clarke, Joseph,	Lists and Returns,	55, 101
Cockran, Christopher	Lists and Returns,	101
Coffin, Christopher,	Gen. Huntington's Note Book.	
Cole, David,	Rec. Conn. Men,	363
	Lists and Returns,	55, 101
Cole, Jesse,	Rec. Conn. Men,	294
Cole, Nathaniel, Corp.,	Hist. New Milford,	218
Comstock, Theophilus,	Lists and Returns,	55, 101
Converse, Damon R.,	Rolls and Lists,	110
Copley, Daniel,	Rec. Conn. Men,	663
Copley, David,	Rec. Conn. Men,	663
Copley, Samuel,	Hist. New Milford,	218
Couch, Ebenezer, Capt.,	Rec. Conn. Men,	391, 492, 583
	Hist. New Milford,	218
Couch, Ebenezer, Jr.,	Rec. Conn. Men,	583
Couch, John, Fifer,	Hist. New Milford,	218
Crane, Stephen,	Hist. New Milford,	689
Crittenden, Jonathan,	Hist. New Milford,	218
Crosley, Prince,	Rec. Conn. Men,	221
Dailey, James,	Lists and Returns,	27, 73, 101, 166
Davenport, Bernard,	Lists and Returns,	106
Davenport, John, Corp.,	Rolls and Lists,	110
Davenport, Squire,	Rec. Conn. Men,	324, 361, 369
Davenport, Theo.,	Lists and Returns,	106
Dean, Caswell,	Hist. New Milford,	218
De Forest, Isaac,	D. A. R. Lin. Book Vol. XVII.,	4
	Rec. Conn. Men,	393
Douglass, Skeen,	Rec. Conn. Men,	323, 364, 370
Drinkwater, Ebenezer,	Lists and Returns,	55, 101
Drinkwater, Henry,	Gen. Huntington's Note Book.	
Drinkwater, Jno.,	Lists and Returns,	187
Drinkwater, Thomas,	Hist. New Milford,	218
Drinkwater, William,	Rec. Conn. Men,	63, 93, 222
	Gen. Huntington's Note Book.	
	Lists and Returns,	27, 55, 74, 101
Dudley, Abisha,	Lists and Returns,	106
Dulford, Alex,	Lists and Returns,	105
Dunning, Ezra,	Hist. New Milford,	218
Dunwell, William,	Lists and Returns,	27, 55, 73, 101, 166
Durkee, Jedediah,	Hist. New Milford,	218
Durkee, Nathaniel,	Lists and Returns,	101
Dye, Daniel,	Lists and Returns,	101

Name	Authority	Page
Edwards, Abel,	Rec. Conn. Men,	65
Eggleston, John, G.,	Rec. Conn. Men,	294
Eustace, Francis,	Lists and Returns,	101
Evitts, Stephen,	Hist. New Milford,	218
Fairchild, Sherman,	Lists and Returns,	202
Farrand, Asa,	Hist. New Milford,	218
Ferriss, Orange,	Rec. Conn. Men,	63
Finkins, Edward,	Rolls and Lists,	106
Fish, John,	Gen. Huntington's Note Book. Lists and Returns,	101
Foot, William,	Hist. New Milford,	218
	Lists and Returns,	55, 101
Frothingham, John,	Lists and Returns,	101
Gaylord, Benjamin,	Rolls and Lists,	21
Gaylord, Ebenezer,	D. A. R. Lin. Book Vol. V.,	256
Giddings, Jonathan,	Hist. New. Milford,	704
Gorham, Phineas,	Rec. Conn. Men,	509
	Hist. New Milford,	405
Gratis, Jesse,	Lists and Returns,	107
Gratis, Prince,	Lists and Returns,	101
Gray, Jonathan,	Hist. New Milford,	218
Gregory, Elnathan,	Hist. New Milford,	218
Gunn, Epenetus,	Hist. New Milford,	218
Hall, Samuel,	Rolls and Lists,	103
Hamblin, William, Jr.,	Rolls and Lists,	23
Hamlin, Benjamin,	Rec. Conn. Men,	653, 663
	Hist. New Milford,	796
Hamlin, Elisha,	Lin. Book Vol. XXIII.,	200
Harrison, Lemuel, Lieut.,	Rec. Conn. Men,	629
Hawkins, Job,	Rec. Conn. Men,	326, 364
Hawley, Joseph C.,	Rolls and Lists,	89
	Lists and Returns,	31, 55, 74, 120
Hawley, Leverius,	Hist. New Milford,	218
	Lists and Returns,	55, 120
Hendricks, Eleazor,	Rec. Conn. Men,	326, 364
	Hist. New Milford,	218
	Lists and Returns,	55, 106
Hine, Noble,	Hist. New Milford,	218
	Lin. Book Vol. XXV.,	318
Hine, Stephen,	Rec. Conn. Men,	513
	Hist. New Milford,	712
Hitchcock, Luke,	D. A. R. Lin. Book Vol. XIX.,	150
Hotchkiss, Asahel,	Hist. New Milford,	218
Hotchkiss, Jared,	Rolls and Lists,	110
Howard, Hiram,	Gen. Huntington's Note Book.	
Hoyt, Elijah,	Rec. Conn. Men,	583
Hubbell, Shadrach, Lieut.,	Rec. Conn. Men,	612
Hunt, Lewis,	Hist. New Milford,	219
Hunt, Theophilus,	Lists and Returns,	188

Name	Authority	Page
Hurd, George,	Rec. Conn. Men,	581
Hurlbut, Reuben,	Rec. Conn. Men,	583
Ingersoll, Briggs,	Rolls and Lists,	110
Jacklin, Thaddeus,	Rolls and Lists,	110
Jackson, Uri,	Hist. New Milford,	218
Johnson, Daniel,	Rec. Conn. Men,	364
Johnson, Richard,	Rec. Conn. Men,	394, 521
	Hist. New Milford,	218
Kane, William,	Rolls and Lists,	102
Keeler, David,	Hist. New Milford,	218
Keeler, Ebenezer,	Lists and Returns,	55, 120
Keeler, John,	Hist. New Milford,	218
Keeler, Nathan,	Hist. New Milford,	218
Knap, John,	Lists and Returns,	55, 105
Lines, Joseph,	Rec. Conn. Men,	103
Lockwood, David,	Rec. Conn. Men,	663
Lockwood, Isaac,	Rec. Conn. Men,	365
Lum, Jonathan,	Hist. New Milford,	218
Maxwell, Caleb,	Rec. Conn. Men,	219
McCoy, John,	Rec. Conn. Men,	365
McDonald, Charles, Sergt.,	Rec. Conn. Men,	326, 364
	Lists and Returns,	55, 120
Mead, Benjamin,	Rec. Conn. Men,	583
Merwin, Andrew,	Rec. Conn. Men,	583
Merwin, David,	Rec. Conn. Men,	583
	Lists and Returns,	55, 105
Merwin, John, Capt.,	Rec. Conn. Men,	523
Middleton, Peter,	Rec. Conn. Men,	180
Miner, Ephraim,	Hist. New Milford,	218
Mix, Elisha,	Lists and Returns,	107
Moger, Abijah,	Lists and Returns,	55, 73, 105
Morgan, Gideon, Corp.,	Hist. New Milford,	218
Mott, Isaac,	Rec. Conn. Men,	294
Mott, Lyman,	Rec. Conn. Men,	294
Munson, Timothy, Sergt.,	Rolls and Lists,	21
Murray, John,	Rolls and Lists,	110
Mygatt, Joseph,	Rec. Conn. Men,	413
	Hist. New Milford,	218
Nearing, Henry,	Rec. Conn. Men,	663
Negro, Shem,	Lists and Returns,	102
Newell, Hanford,	Rolls and Lists,	110
Nichols, Ely,	Rec. Conn. Men,	224
	Lists and Returns,	55, 105
Nichols, Garshom,	Lists and Returns,	55, 105
Nichols, Robert,	Lists and Returns,	101
Nichols, Samuel,	Rolls and Lists,	110
Nichols, William, Corp.,	Hist. New Milford,	218

Name	Authority	Page
Noble, Gideon, Sergt.,	Hist. New Milford,	743
Noble, Goodman,	Lists and Returns,	55, 105
Noble, Lyman,	Hist. New Milford,	218
Noble, Morgan, 2nd, Lieut.,	Rec. Conn. Men,	61
Noble, Zadock,	Rev. Sol. Scrap Book,	42
Northrop, Amos,	Hist. New Milford,	602, 747
Osborn, Nathaniel,	Rec. Conn. Men,	115, 298
Palmer, Chileab,	Lists and Returns,	55, 101
Palmer, Ichabod B.,	Lists and Returns,	123
Palmer, Thomas,	Rolls and Lists,	104, 131
Peet, Lemuel,	Lists and Returns,	37, 55, 73, 101, 173
Peet, William,	Hist. New Milford,	218
Phelps, William,	Hist. New Milford,	750
	Rec. Conn. Men,	394
Phillips, Israel,	Lists and Returns,	101
Philips, Jeruel,	Lists and Returns,	55
Philips, Reuben,	Hist. New Milford,	218
Philips, Samuel,	Lists and Returns,	55, 101
	Rec. Conn. Men,	225
Philips, Shubel,	Lists and Returns,	55, 101
Porter, David, Sergt.,	Hist. New Milford,	218
	Rec. Conn. Men,	294
Porter, Nathaniel,	Rolls and Lists,	110
Prime, Amos,	Hist. New Milford,	218
Prince, Samuel,	Hist. New Milford,	218
Purdey, Jesse,	Lists and Returns,	173
Randall, Charles,	Rec. Conn. Men,	663
Randall, Timothy,	Hist. New Milford,	753
Read, Asa,	Rec. Conn. Men,	583
Robards, Aziah,	Hist. New Milford,	218
Rogers, Daniel,	Lists and Returns,	55, 105
Rood, John,	Hist. New Milford,	218
Rowley, Nathan,	Hist. New Milford,	218
Ruggles, Benjamin,	Rolls and Lists,	110
Ruggles, Bostwick,	Rec. Conn. Men,	365
Ruggles, David, Fifer,	Hist. New Milford,	218, 300, 757
Ruggles, Isaac,	Hist. New Milford,	218
Ruggles, Joseph,	Rolls and Lists,	24
Ruggles, Lazarus, Capt.,	Rec. Conn. Men,	667
Rush, George,	Lists and Returns,	105
Sanford, David,	D. A. R. Lin. Book Vol. XVI.,	103
Sanford, Liffe, Sergt.,	Rec. Conn. Men,	219, 326
	Hist. New Milford,	426
	Lists and Returns,	55, 105
Sanford, Nehemiah,	Hist. New Milford,	431, 760
Sax, Othniel,	Lists and Returns,	106, 120
Seelye, Benjamin, Lieut.,	Hist. New Milford,	220
	Rec. Conn. Men,	629

New Milford

Name	Authority	Page
Sheldon, Job, Sergt.,	Rec. Conn. Men,	636
Sherman, David,	Lists and Returns,	105
Sherman, John,	D. A. R. Lin. Book Vol. XXI.,	213
Smith, Levi,	Rec. Conn. Men,	663
Smith, Ralph,	Lists and Returns,	55, 105
Smith, Robert,	Lists and Returns,	101
Smith, Samuel,	Lists and Returns,	107
Starkweather, Asa,	Hist. New Milford,	218
Starr, Eli,	Rolls and Lists,	52
Starr, Elijah, Ensign,	Rec Conn. Men,	586
Starr, Josiah, Col.,	Rec. Conn. Men,	61
	Hist. New Milford,	224, 276
	Lists and Returns,	41, 73, 175
Steward, Mathew,	Rec. Conn. Men,	364
Stillwell, Ebenezer,	Rec. Conn. Men,	364
Stillwell, Stephen, alias Allen,	Rec. Conn. Men,	226
	Lists and Returns,	41, 73, 100, 175
Stone, Benjamin,	Rec. Conn. Men,	548
Stone, Julius,	Rec. Conn. Men,	492
Straight, Henry,	Rec. Conn. Men,	583
Summers, David, (Bridgewater)	Biographical Rev. of L'f'd. County,	62
Taylor, Augustine, Lieut.,	Rec. Conn. Men,	217, 218, 527
Taylor, Simeon,	Rec. Conn. Men,	583
(A Litchfield man who went as substitute was of that name).		
Terrel, Job,	Lists and Returns,	187
Terrell, Stephen,	Hist. New Milford,	219, 776
Terrill, James,		
Thayer, Lemuel, Corp.,	Hist. New Milford,	218
Todd, Jonah,	Hist. New Milford,	218
Tomlinson, Jabez,	Rec. Conn. Men,	279, 283
Treat, Mingo,	Rec. Conn. Men,	226
	Lists and Returns,	55
Trowbridge, Ebenezer,	Hist. New Milford,	219
	Lists and Returns,	42, 55, 105, 176
Trowbridge, William P.,	Rolls and Lists,	67
Turner, John,	Rec. Conn. Men,	294
Turner, Samuel,	Rec. Conn. Men,	294
Turrill, Ashael,	Rec. Conn. Men,	105, 238
	Hist. New Milford,	776
Turrill, Ashael,	Rec. Conn. Men,	294
Turrill, John,	Rec. Conn. Men,	167
	Hist. New Milford,	218
Utter, Isaac,	Rolls and Lists,	82
Videto, Joseph,	Lists and Returns,	186
Wagner, John,	Rec. Conn. Men,	663
Warner, Elizur, Lieut.,	Hist. New Milford,	218
Warner, Solomon,	Rolls and Lists,	110

Name	Authority	Page
Weeks, James,	Lists and Returns,	101
Welch, Luke,	Lists and Returns,	101
Welch, Michael,	Rolls and Lists,	83
Weller, Benjamin, Sergt.,	Hist. New Milford,	218
Weller, Cooley,	Hist. New Milford,	219
Wharton, Benjamin,	Hist. New Milford,	225, 789
Wharton, Joseph,	Hist. New Milford,	225
Wharton, Solomon,	Rec. Conn. Men,	621
	Hist. New Milford,	789
Wheeler, Abraham,	Lists and Returns,	123
Wheeler, Stephen, Sergt.,	Rolls and Lists,	68
	Lists and Returns,	55, 105
Whiteley, William,	Hist. New Milford,	219
	Lists and Returns,	5, 55, 105, 177
Whittlesey, David, Sergt.,	Hist. New Milford,	218
Wildman, Matthew,	Hist. New Milford,	219
	Lists and Returns,	55, 101
Wildman, Nathan,	Rolls and Lists,	91
Wilkinson, Abel,	Rec. Conn. Men,	294
	Hist. New Milford,	219
Wilkinson, Ichabod,	Rec. Conn. Men,	226
(Wilkeson)	Hist. New Milford,	224
	Lists and Returns,	55, 74, 105
Wilkinson, Jonathan,	Rec. Conn. Men,	294
Wilkinson, Peter,	Lists and Returns,	202
Williams, Ebenezer,	Hist. New Milford,	219
Williams, Henry,	Lists and Returns,	107
Wilson, James,	Lists and Returns,	101
Wilson, Javan, (colored)	Rec. Conn. Men,	637
Wilson, Nathaniel,	Rec. Conn. Men,	663
Wooster, Truman,	Lists and Returns,	101
Worden, Joseph,	Rec. Conn. Men,	63

Supplemental List as recorded in
"TWO CENTURIES OF NEW MILFORD, 1707-1907."

Colonel Andrew Ward's Regiment of Connecticut Militia, as given In Orcutt's New Milford:

Stephen Turrill, Abel Wilkins.

Captain Isaac Bostwick's Company, 6th Regiment:

Lieutenant Hulbutt,
Sergt. Simeon Porter,
Sergt. Simon Mills,
Sergt. Solomon Barnum,
Corp. Harmon White,
Corp. Ebenezer Barnum,

Corp. Seth Hall,
Drummer Calvin Pease,
Fifer Nathan Avery,
Fifer Theodore Baldwin,
Fifer David Roach.

Privates:

Joseph Bates,
Reuben Bellamy,
Jonathan Brown,
Asahel Case,
Thadeus Cole,
Timothy Cole,
John D. Comstock,
[1]Hedekiah Clark,
Joseph Clark,
Aaron Curtis,
Asahel Dean,
Jeremiah Douchey,
David Everist,
James Gates,
Hedekiah Gray,
John Green,
Daniel Grinnel,
Amaziah Griswold,
Levit How,
William Hale,
Abner Kelsey,
John Lewis,
Simon Lyman,

David Lyons,
Reuben Mager,
Samuel Millar,
Josiah Munger,
Joseph Murray,
Phineas Palmer,
Rufus Partridge,
Jeruel Philips,
Howard E. Prince,
Cordeal Smith,
Isaac Smith,
John Smith,
Caleb Swetland,
Absolom Taylor,
Reuben Taylor,
Gamaliel Terrey,
Benjamin Thomas,
Job Tousley,
John Walter,
Samuel Waters,
Cornelius Whitney,
Thomas Woodward,

[1] Found in more than one place in this list.

Men who crossed the Delaware with Capt. Isaac Bostwick, and were in the Battle of Trenton, and the succeeding Battle of Princeton, Jan. 3, 1777:

Corp. Bell,
Corp. Grover,
Fifer Humstead,

Fifer Jeptha Bartholemew,
Fifer Luther Bartholemew,

Privates:

Isaac Brownson,
Moses Camp,
Moses Canfield,
¹Hedekiah Clark,
William Cressey,
Jonathan Davidson,
Francis Fields,
Aaron Foot,

Moses Hurd,
Robert Nichols,
George Norton,
Elisha Phinney,
Reuben Pitcher,
Asa Prince,
Wills Sherwood,

Men who served in the 6th Company of 4th Regiment.

Ephraim Alderman,
Dar. Barnes,
Amos Beach,
Michael Beach,
Asa Beal,
William Beal,
Josiah Brooks,
James Brown,
Robt. Brown,
Domini Douglass,
Jabez Frisbie,
Elihu Grant,
Christo. Hington,
Levi Hunt,
Geo. Lummis,
Jonathan Mayo,
Jere McCarte,
Amos McKinnee,

Nathan Nicholas,
Lemuel Peete,
Jos. Phelps,
Oliver Phelps,
Enos Scott,
John Seeley,
Zimri Skinner,
Benajah Smith,
Geo. A. Smith,
Timothy Stanley,
John Stevens,
Nathl. Stewart,
Heman Swift,
Joseph Thair,
Ezekiel Towner,
John Tuff,
Lem Walter,

Men who served in Lieutenant-Colonel Josiah Starr's Regiment:

William Handy,
Titus Hart,
Stephen Headges,
Benjamin Heart,
James Higgins,
Ira Hotchkiss,
Sep Hubble,
Pripe Hubble,
Aaron Hull,

Holan Nettleton,
Samuel Nettleton,
¹Robert Nichols,
Elab Parker,
Elijah Parker,
¹Jurel Phillips,
Nehemiah Piffany,
Augustine Thayer,

¹ Found in more than one place in this list.

Men who were in Lieutenant-Colonel Samuel Canfield's Regiment of Connecticut Militia at West Point, 1781:

Stephen Bennett.

Men who served in Connecticut Regiment of Pioneers:

Col. Judthon Baldwin,
Capt. Daniel Pendleton,

Isaac Turrill,
Samuel Oviatt, (Rev. Sol. Scrap Book).

Men who served in Capt. Moses Hazen's Regiment:

Michael Welch.

Men who served in Capt. Belden's Company:

David Johnson,

Moses Scott.

Men in General David Waterbury's State Regiment, Capt. Charles Smith's Company:

Sergt. Josiah Barnes,

Fifer Oliver Mead.

Privates:

Jonathan Beecher,
Benton Buck,
John Ingersoll,

Jonathan Jessup.
Nathan Murray,
John Warner,

Men in Col. Benjamin Hinman's Fourth Regiment, Capt. Josiah Starr:

John Stevens,
Asa Brownson,

[1]Josiah Brooks.

Men who served under Lieut-Colonel Canfield in the Tryon invasion:

Nathaniel Barnes,
William Cogswell,

Adam Hurlburt.

---

[1] Found in more than one place in this list.

Norfolk

Revolutionary Soldiers

OF

Norfolk

COMPILED BY
GREEN WOODS CHAPTER
DAUGHTERS OF THE AMERICAN REVOLUTION
WINSTED, CONN.

For fuller accounts of these men see original lists

Revolutionary Soldiers of Norfolk

Name	Authority	Page
Abernathy, Jared,	Rec. Conn. Men,	18
	Rolls and Lists,	39
	Hist. Norfolk,	82, 86
Adams, Asahel, (Asa)	Rec. Conn. Men,	220, 229
	Lists and Returns,	21, 74, 177
	Hist. Norfolk,	84
Aspinwall, Aaron,	Rec. Conn. Men,	220
	Hist. Norfolk,	84, 88
	Lists and Returns,	22, 74, 177
Aspinwall, Caleb,	Rec. Conn. Men,	18, 63
	Rolls and Lists,	39
	Hist. Norfolk,	81, 84
	Lists and Returns,	22, 74, 177
Atwater, Ichabod,	Rec. Conn. Men,	523, 664
	Hist. Norfolk,	90
Bale, Hendrick, (Bail)	Rec. Conn. Men,	331, 353
*Barber, Timothy, Capt., (Barbor)	Rec. Conn. Men,	612
Barden, Abraham,	Hist. Norfolk,	86
	Lists and Returns,	210
Barnum, Levi,	Hist. Norfolk,	83, 96
	Rec. Conn. Men,	93
Beach, Abraham,	Rec. Conn. Men,	18
	Hist. Norfolk,	82, 83
Beach, John, Sergt.,	Rec. Conn. Men,	407
	Hist. Norfolk,	85, 91
*Berkley, Richard,	Rec. Conn. Men,	664
	Hist. Norfolk,	90
Benedict, James,	Rec. Conn. Men,	220, 650
	Hist. Norfolk,	89
	Lists and Returns,	74
Benedict, James, Jr.,	Hist. Norfolk,	84
	Hist. Litchfield Co.,	472
Bingham, Ozias,	Rec. Conn. Men,	61
	Hist. Norfolk,	82
Bishop, Bela, (Bille)	Rec. Conn. Men,	562
	Hist. Norfolk,	91
Bradley, John, Capt.,	Hist. Norfolk,	527
Brown, Ephraim,	Rec. Conn. Men,	664
	Hist. Norfolk,	90
Brown, Titus,	Rec. Conn. Men,	18, 459, 489
	Hist. Norfolk,	82, 87, 89
Butler, Isaac,	Rec. Conn. Men,	46, 228
	Rolls and Lists,	39
	Hist. Norfolk,	86, 91
	Lists and Returns,	209

Name	Authority	Page
Cady, Charles,	Rec. Conn. Men,	583
Camp, Moses,	Rec. Conn. Men,	105
	D. A. R. Lin. Book Vol. XXIII.,	58
Camp, Samuel, Ensign,	Rec. Conn. Men,	8
Canfield, Daniel,	Hist. Norfolk,	85
	Hist. Litchfield Co.,	473
Case, Asahel,	Hist. Norfolk,	91
	Rolls and Lists,	39
Case, Asahel, Jr.,	Hist. Norfolk,	91
Cole, Silas,	Rec. Conn. Men,	261
	Hist. Norfolk,	91
Cowles, Amasa, Sr.,	Hist. Norfolk,	517
Cowles, Daniel,	Rec. Conn. Men,	290
Cowles, Noah,	Hist. Norfolk,	86
	Hist. Litchfield Co.,	473
Cowles, Samuel, Sergt.,	Rec. Conn. Men,	18
	Hist. Norfolk,	81, 86, 516
	Hist. Litchfield Co.,	473
Cowles, Silas,	Hist. Norfolk,	85
	Hist. Litchfield Co.,	472
	Lists and Returns,	74
Coy, Ephraim,	Rec. Conn. Men,	73, 148, 653
	Hist. Norfolk,	88
Curtiss, Solomon,	Rec. Conn. Men,	495
	Hist. Norfolk,	84, 88
Curtiss, Thomas,	Rec. Conn. Men,	18
	Hist. Norfolk,	81, 84
Darrah, James,	Rec. Conn. Men,	261
Dunbar, Salathiel,	Rec. Conn. Men,	61
	Hist. Norfolk,	84
Field, Joseph,	Rec. Conn. Men,	583
Field, Nathaniel,	Rec. Conn. Men,	18
	Rolls and Lists,	39
	Hist. Norfolk,	82, 83
French, William,	Rec. Conn. Men,	562
	Hist. Norfolk,	91
Frisbie, Luther,	Rec. Conn. Men,	290
Fuller, Edward,	Rec. Conn. Men,	222, 634
	Rolls and Lists,	39
	Hist. Norfolk,	85, 88
	Lists and Returns,	74
Gaylord, ———,	Hist. Norfolk,	86
	Hist. Litchfield Co.,	473
Gaylord, Ambrose,	Rec. Conn. Men,	317
	Hist. Norfolk,	86
Gaylord, Giles, Lieut.,	Rec. Conn. Men,	63, 627
	Hist. Norfolk,	85, 90
Gaylord, Ludd,	Hist. Norfolk,	86
	Hist. Litchfield Co.,	473
Gaylord, Timothy, Capt.,	Rec. Conn. Men,	18, 395
	Hist. Norfolk,	81, 87

NORFOLK 139

Name	Authority	Page
Gaylord, Timothy, 2nd,	Rec. Conn. Men,	18
	Hist. Norfolk,	82, 87
Gaylord, Royce,	Hist. Norfolk,	514
*Grant, Roswell,	Hist. Norfolk,	86, 556
	Annals of Winchester,	176
	Hist. Litchfield Co.,	473
*Guiteau, Ephraim, Dr.,	Hist. Norfolk,	481, 565
Hall, Hiland, (Highland)	Rec. Conn. Men,	143
	Hist. Norfolk,	84
	Lists and Returns,	74
Hall, Joseph,	Hist. Norfolk,	91
Hamlin, Joel,	Rec. Conn. Men,	223
	Hist. Norfolk,	84
	Rolls and Lists,	39
	Lists and Returns,	32, 74, 169
Heady, David,	Rec. Conn. Men,	664
	Hist. Norfolk,	85
Hewet, William, Clerk,	Rec. Conn. Men,	18
	Hist. Norfolk,	81, 87
Holt, Elezear,	Hist. Norfolk,	83
	Hist. Litchfield Co.,	472
Holt, Nicholas,	Rec. Conn. Men,	649
	Rolls and Lists,	39
	Hist. Norfolk,	84, 88, 91
Holt, Stephen,	Hist. Norfolk,	84, 561
	Hist. Litchfield Co.,	472
Hoskins, Daniel,	Rec. Conn. Men,	470
	Hist. Norfolk,	85, 89
*Hosmer, Thomas, Capt.,	Hist. Norfolk,	517
Hotchkiss, Josiah,	Rec. Conn. Men,	61
	Hist. Norfolk,	88
	Hist. Litchfield Co.,	472, 473
Hotchkiss, Samuel,	Rec. Conn. Men,	18
	Hist. Norfolk,	83, 88
	Hist. Litchfield Co.,	472, 473
Hotchkiss, Samuel, Jr.,	Rec. Conn. Men,	18
	Hist. Norfolk,	81, 88
How, John,	Rec. Conn. Men,	586
Hoyt, Ebenezer,	Rec. Conn. Men,	18
	Hist. Norfolk,	81, 87
Hubbard, Jonas,	Rec. Conn. Men,	223, 366, 639
	Hist. Norfolk,	85, 89
	Hist. Litchfield Co.,	472
	Lists and Returns,	74
Hull, Jehiel,	Rec. Conn. Men,	61
	Hist. Norfolk,	83
	Hist. Litchfield Co.,	472
	Lists and Returns,	209
Humphrey, Asahel,	Rec. Conn. Men,	124
	Hist. Norfolk,	78, 565
Ives, Titus, 1st Lieut., Capt.,	Rec. Conn. Men,	542
	Hist. Norfolk,	90
	D. A. R. Lin. Book Vol. XXVIII.,	22

140 LITCHFIELD COUNTY REVOLUTIONARY SOLDIERS

Name	Authority	Page
Jones, Joseph,	Rec. Conn. Men,	61
	Rolls and Lists,	39
	Hist. Norfolk,	512, 513
*Kirkham, Philemon,	Annals of Winchester,	342, 343, 344
Knapp, Abraham, (Knap)	Rec. Conn. Men,	223
	Rolls and Lists,	39
	Hist. Norfolk,	84
	Lists and Returns,	74
Knapp, Elijah, Corp., (Knap)	Rec. Conn. Men,	223
	Hist. Norfolk,	84, 88
	Hist. Litchfield Co.,	472
	Lists and Returns,	79
Lawrence, Arial,	Hist. Norfolk,	85
	Hist. Litchfield Co.,	473
Lawrence, Luther,	Rec. Conn. Men,	203
	Hist. Norfolk,	86, 89
	Hist. Litchfield Co.,	473
	Lists and Returns,	205
Leach, William,	Rec. Conn. Men,	228
	Hist. Norfolk,	86
	Hist. Litchfield Co.,	473
	Lists and Returns,	209
Lester, Andrew,	Rec. Conn. Men,	18
	Hist. Norfolk,	81, 83, 88
	Hist. Litchfield Co.,	472
Mack, Ebenezer,	Rec. Conn. Men,	93
	Hist. Norfolk,	83
	Hist. Litchfield Co.,	472
Mars, Jupiter,	Hist. Norfolk,	91, 370
Mason, Elijah,	Rec. Conn. Men,	562
	Hist. Norfolk,	91
Mills, Constantine,	Hist. Norfolk,	89
	Mills Genealogy,	32
Mills, Eden,	Hist. Norfolk,	83
	Hist. Litchfield Co.,	472
Mills, Michael, Capt.,	Rolls and Lists,	214
	Hist. Norfolk,	87
	Hist. Litchfield Co.,	473
Mills, Simeon, Sergt.,	Rec. Conn. Men,	82
	Rolls and Lists,	265
	Hist. Norfolk,	85, 86, 89
Minor, John, (Miner)	Rec. Conn. Men,	228
	Hist. Norfolk,	86
	Lists and Returns,	209
Minor, Justis,	Rec. Conn. Men,	583
Moor, Andrew,	Rolls and Lists,	39
	Hist. Norfolk,	86
	Hist. Litchfield Co.,	473
Munger, Elizur,	Hist. Norfolk,	85
	Hist. Litchfield Co.,	473
Munger, Reuben,	Hist. Norfolk,	85
	Hist. Litchfield Co.,	473

NORFOLK 141

Name	Authority	Page
Murray, Jasper, (Murry)	Rec. Conn. Men,	61, 542
	Hist. Norfolk,	83, 88
Murray, Jeoffrey,	Rec. Conn. Men,	18
	Hist. Norfolk,	81, 87
	Hist. Litchfield Co.,	473
Noble, Peter,	Rec. Conn. Men,	93
	Hist. Norfolk,	83
	Hist. Litchfield Co.,	472
Norton, Levi,	Rec. Conn. Men,	635
	Hist. Norfolk,	84, 88
	Hist. Litchfield Co.,	472
	Lists and Returns,	74
Norton, Lewis,	Rec. Conn. Men,	583
Norton, Phineas,	Rec. Conn. Men,	18
	Hist. Norfolk,	82, 87
	Hist. Litchfield Co.,	473
Orvis, David, (Orris)	Rec. Conn. Men,	18
	Hist. Norfolk,	82, 87
	Hist. Litchfield Co.,	473
Orvis, Elezear,	Lists and Returns,	36
Orvis, Eliezer, (Orris)	Hist. Norfolk,	85
	Hist. Litchfield Co.,	472
Orvis, Roger, (Orris)	Rec. Conn. Men,	61, 639
	Rolls and Lists,	39
	Hist. Norfolk,	83, 88
Orvis, Samuel, (Orris)	Rec. Conn. Men,	643
	Hist. Norfolk,	84, 88
	Hist. Litchfield Co.,	472
	Lists and Returns,	74
Palmer, Reuben,	Rec. Conn. Men,	664
	Hist. Norfolk,	90
Parker, Ephraim,	Rec. Conn. Men,	18
	Hist. Norfolk,	81, 87
	Hist. Litchfield Co.,	473
Parker, Jotham,	Hist. Norfolk,	83
	Hist. Litchfield Co.,	472
Pettibone, Daniel,	Rec. Conn. Men,	61
	Hist. Norfolk,	83, 91
	Hist. Litchfield Co.,	472
Pettibone, Eli,	Hist. Norfolk,	86
	Hist. Litchfield Co.,	473
Pettibone, Elijah,	Rec. Conn. Men,	18, 562
	Rolls and Lists,	39
	Hist. Norfolk,	81, 87, 91
Pettibone, Giles,	Rec. Conn. Men,	437
	Hist. Norfolk,	87
	Hist. Litchfield Co.,	473
	D. A. R. Lin. Book Vol. XXIII.,	199
Pettibone, Samuel, Lieut.,	Rec. Conn. Men,	418
	Hist. Norfolk,	87, 89
	Hist. Litchfield Co.,	473
Phelps, ———, Lieut.,	Hist. Norfolk,	85
	Hist. Litchfield Co.,	473

142   LITCHFIELD COUNTY REVOLUTIONARY SOLDIERS

Name	Authority	Page
Phelps, Darius,	Rec. Conn. Men,	63
	Hist. Norfolk,	83
	Hist. Litchfield Co.,	472
Phelps, Elijah,	Rec. Conn. Men,	352
	Hist. Norfolk,	86, 91
	Hist. Litchfield Co.,	473
Phelps, Jeremiah Wilcox,	Rec. Conn. Men,	562
	Hist. Norfolk,	91
	Hist. Litchfield Co.,	473
Phelps, Joseph,	Rec. Conn. Men,	562
	Hist. Norfolk,	91
Plumb, Amariah,	Rec. Conn. Men,	18
	Hist. Norfolk,	82, 83
	Hist. Litchfield Co.,	472
	Lists and Returns,	37, 74
Plumbley, Ebenezer,	Rec. Conn. Men,	418
(Plumley)	Hist. Norfolk,	85, 90
	Hist. Litchfield Co.,	473
*Porter, John, Capt.,	Rec. Conn. Men,	625
Richards, Jedediah,	Rec. Conn. Men,	405, 542
	Hist. Norfolk,	90
Richards, Jedediah, Jr.,	Hist. Norfolk,	85
	Hist. Litchfield Co.,	473
Riggs, Miles,	Rec. Conn. Men,	542
	Hist. Norfolk,	91, 93, 542
Robbins, A. R., Rev.,	Rec. Conn. Men,	110
	Hist. Norfolk,	82, 392
	Hist. Litchfield Co.,	472
*Rockwell, Joseph,	Rec. Conn. Men,	538, 664
	Hist. Norfolk,	90
Rogers, Abithar,	Hist. Norfolk,	90
	Hist. Litchfield Co.,	473
Sets, Allen,	Rec. Conn. Men,	583
Seward, Brotherton,	Rec. Conn. Men,	18, 50
(Seaward)	Rolls and Lists,	39
	Hist. Norfolk,	81, 87, 88
Seward, Elnathan,	Rec. Conn. Men,	219
	Hist. Norfolk,	84
	Hist. Litchfield Co.,	472
	Lists and Returns,	74, 209
Seward, Silas, (Steward)	Rolls and Lists,	39
	Hist. Norfolk,	86
	Hist. Litchfield Co.,	473
Smith, Asher,	Rolls and Lists,	37
	Hist. Norfolk,	85
	Hist. Litchfield Co.,	473
Sperry, Lemuel,	Rec. Conn. Men,	251
	Hist. Norfolk,	85
	Hist. Litchfield Co.,	472
	Lists and Returns,	74
Spencer, John,	Rec. Conn. Men,	583
Stevens, Reuben,	Rolls and Lists,	97
	Hist. Norfolk,	84
	Hist. Litchfield Co.,	472
	Lists and Returns,	74

Name	Authority	Page
Strong, Arial,	Rec. Conn. Men,	203
	Hist. Norfolk,	86
	Hist. Litchfield Co.,	473
	Lists and Returns,	206
Strong, John,	Rec. Conn. Men,	664
	Hist. Norfolk,	90, 95
Sturtevant, Caleb,	Rec. Conn. Men,	225, 644
(Sturduvant)	Hist. Norfolk,	84, 88
	Hist. Litchfield Co.,	472
Sturtevant, James,	Rec. Conn. Men,	228
	Hist. Norfolk,	86
	Hist. Litchfield Co.,	473
	Lists and Returns,	209
Sturtevant, Nathan,	Lists and Returns,	41
Taylor, Samuel,	Rec. Conn. Men,	228
	Hist. Norfolk,	86
	Hist. Litchfield Co.,	473
	Lists and Returns,	210
Thrall, Giles,	Rec. Conn. Men,	227
	Hist. Norfolk,	86
	Hist. Litchfield Co.,	473
Tibbals, Elin,	Rec. Conn. Men,	664
Tibbals, Samuel,	Rec. Conn. Men,	627
	Hist. Norfolk,	85, 90
	Hist. Litchfield Co.,	472
Tibbals, Thomas,	Rec. Conn. Men,	113
	Hist. Norfolk,	85, 533, 534
	Hist. Litchfield Co.,	472
Toby, Jesse, (Jese)	Rec. Conn. Men,	61, 536
	Hist. Norfolk,	33, 88
	Hist. Litchfield Co.,	472
Trall, Rufus, (Thrall)	Rec. Conn. Men,	227
	Rolls and Lists,	39
	Hist. Norfolk,	84
	Lists and Returns,	74
Trowbridge, John, Corp.,	Rec. Conn. Men,	61
	Hist. Norfolk,	84
	Hist. Litchfield Co.,	472
	Lists and Returns,	74
Tubbs, Nathan,	Rec. Conn. Men,	226
	Rolls and Lists,	39
	Hist. Norfolk,	84
	Lists and Returns,	42, 74
Turner, Bates,	Rec. Conn. Men,	228
	Hist. Norfolk,	85
	Hist. Litchfield Co.,	472
	Lists and Returns,	74, 210
Turner, Moses, Corp.,	Rec. Conn. Men,	219, 640
	Rolls and Lists,	39
	Hist. Norfolk,	84, 88
	Lists and Returns,	74
Turner, William,	Rec. Conn. Men,	644
	Hist. Norfolk,	85, 88
	Hist. Litchfield Co.,	472
	Lists and Returns,	74

Name	Authority	Page
Tuttle, Benjamin,	Rec. Conn. Men,	18
	Hist. Norfolk,	82, 87
	Hist. Litchfield Co.,	473
Walter, Charles,	Rec. Conn. Men,	335, 638
	Rolls and Lists,	39
	Hist. Norfolk,	83, 88
	Lists and Returns,	74
Walter, John,	Rec. Conn. Men,	644
	Hist. Norfolk,	84, 88
	Hist. Litchfield Co.,	472
	Lists and Returns,	74
Warner, John,	Rec. Conn. Men,	290
Watson, Heman,	Rolls and Lists,	39
	Hist. Norfolk,	89
Watson, Titus, Capt.,	Rec. Conn. Men,	18
	Rolls and Lists,	39
	Hist. Norfolk,	81, 84, 88
	Lists and Returns,	44, 79
Welch, Hopestill,	Hist. Norfolk,	84, 466
	Hist. Litchfield Co.,	472
	Stiles Ancient Windsor Vol. II.,	783
White, Daniel, (Matthew)	Rec. Conn. Men,	664
	Hist. Norfolk,	90
	See Torrington List.	
White, Jedediah,	Rec. Conn. Men,	638
	Hist. Norfolk,	83
	Hist. Litchfield Co.,	472
Wilcox, Hosea, Capt.,	Rec. Conn. Men,	646
	Hist. Norfolk,	48, 551
Wright, Freedom,	Rec. Conn. Men,	18
	Boyd's Annals,	265
	Hist. Norfolk,	82, 83

Plymouth and Thomaston

Revolutionary Soldiers

OF

Plymouth and Thomaston

COMPILED BY
ABI HUMASTON CHAPTER
DAUGHTERS OF THE AMERICAN REVOLUTION
THOMASTON, CONN.

Revolutionary Soldiers of Plymouth and Thomaston

Name	Authority	Page
Adkins, David,	Rec. Conn. Men,	663
Allen, Ebenezer,	Rec. Conn. Men,	160, 632
	Hist. Waterbury Vol. I.,	460
Allen, John,	Rec. Conn. Men,	395, 613
Atwater, Isaac,	Year Book S. A. R. 1895-96,	483
Barnes, Nathaniel, Capt.,	Rec. Conn. Men,	96, 522, 548, 624
Bartholomew, Daniel,	Rec. Conn. Men,	6
Beach, Thaddeus,	Rec. Conn. Men,	633
	Hist. Waterbury Vol. I.,	461
Blakeslee, Joel,	Hist. Waterbury Vol. I.,	461
Bunnell, Hezekiah,	Rec. Conn. Men,	396, 620
Bunnell, Titus, Capt.,	Rec. Conn. Men,	395, 629
Camp, Samuel, Capt.,	Rec. Conn. Men,	8, 43, 231, 391, 435, 501, 547
Conant, Roger, Dr.,	Rec. Conn. Men,	395
	Hist. Waterbury Vol. I.,	462
Cook, Charles,	Hist. Waterbury Vol. I.,	462
	Rec. Conn. Men,	612
Cook, Ebenezer,	Rec. Conn. Men,	117, 612
Cook, Lemuel,	D. A. R. Lin. Book Vol. XXIII.,	292
	Hist. Waterbury Vol. I.,	282, 641
Curtis, Isaac,	Rec. Conn. Men,	500
	Hist. Waterbury Vol. I.,	462
Curtis, James,	Rec. Conn. Men,	612
	Hist. Waterbury Vol. I.,	462
Curtis, Jotham, Capt.,	Rec. Conn. Men,	522, 548, 612, 624
Curtis, Samuel,	Rec. Conn. Men,	612
	Hist. Waterbury Vol. I.,	462
Curtis, Stephen,	Rec. Conn. Men,	232, 612
	Hist. Waterbury Vol. I.,	462
Darrow, Ebenezer,	Rec. Conn. Men,	274
	Hist. Waterbury Vol. I.,	462
Doolittle, Eben,	App. for Pension.	
Dunbar, Aaron,	Rec. Conn. Men,	612
	Hist. Waterbury Vol. I.,	462
Dunbar, John,	Rec. Conn. Men,	612
	Hist. Waterbury Vol. I.,	462
Dunbar, Joseph,	Rec. Conn. Men,	117, 648, 667
	Hist. Waterbury Vol. I.,	462
Evans, Randol,	Rec. Conn. Men,	612
	Hist. Waterbury Vol. I.,	462
Faucher, Ithiel,	Rec. Conn. Men,	535, 612
	Hist. Waterbury Vol. I.,	462

Name	Authority	Page
Faucher, John,	Rec. Conn. Men,	612
Fenn, Aaron,	Hist. Waterbury Vol. I.,	462
Fenn, Eben,	Rec. Conn. Men,	396
Fenn, Jacob,	Rec. Conn. Men,	43
	Hist. Waterbury Vol. I.,	462
	D. A. R. Lin. Book Vol. XXVII.,	67
Fenn, Jason,	Rec. Conn. Men,	43, 612
	Hist. Waterbury Vol. I.,	462
Foot, David,	Rec. Conn. Men,	41, 612
Griggs, Samuel,	Rec. Conn. Men,	612
	Hist. Waterbury Vol. I.,	463
Griggs, Solomon,	Rec. Conn. Men,	41, 500
	Hist. Waterbury Vol. I.,	463
Hitchcock, Zachariah,	Rec. Conn. Men,	612, 628
	Hist. Waterbury Vol. I.,	463
Humiston, David,	Rec. Conn. Men,	612
	Hist. Waterbury Vol. I.,	463
Humiston, Jesse,	Rec. Conn. Men,	43, 658
(Thomaston)	Hist. Waterbury Vol. I.,	464
	D. A. R. Lin. Book Vol. XXVI.,	29
Ives, Elnathan,	Rec. Conn. Men,	24
Lewis, Samuel,	Rec. Conn. Men,	206, 444, 635
	Hist. Waterbury Vol. I.,	464
Markham, Jeremiah,	Rec. Conn. Men,	513, 647
Matthews, Aaron,	Rec. Conn. Men,	41, 116
	Hist. Waterbury Vol. I.,	464
Painter, Thomas,	Rec. Conn. Men,	408
Penfield, Samuel,	Rec. Conn. Men,	612
	Hist. Waterbury Vol. I.,	465
Pond, Bartholomew,	Rec. Conn. Men,	117, 612
	Hist. Waterbury Vol. I.,	465
Pond, Timothy,	Rec. Conn. Men,	41, 236, 612
	Hist. Waterbury Vol. I.,	465
Potter, Daniel,	Rec. Conn. Men,	157, 159, 335, 397
	Hist. Waterbury Vol. I.,	465
Potter, Elinkim,	Rec. Conn. Men,	612
	Hist. Waterbury Vol. I.,	465
Potter, Lake,	Rec. Conn. Men,	500
	Hist. Waterbury Vol. I.,	465
Reynolds, Samuel,	Rec. Conn. Men,	200
	Hist. Waterbury Vol. I.,	465
Rice, Nehemiah,	Rec. Conn. Men,	116, 229, 230, 345
	Hist. Waterbury Vol. I.,	465
Royce, Phineas,	Rec. Conn. Men,	612
	Hist. Waterbury Vol. I.,	465
Sanford, Daniel,	Rec. Conn. Men,	424, 493
	Hist. Waterbury Vol. I.,	465
Sanford, Ezekiel,	Rec. Conn. Men,	70, 184, 393
	Hist. Waterbury Vol. I.,	465
Sanford, Joel,	Rec. Conn. Men,	574, 612
	Hist. Waterbury Vol. I.,	465

Plymouth and Thomaston 151

Name	Authority	Page
Scovil, Samuel,	Rec. Conn. Men,	407, 612, 657
	Hist. Waterbury Vol. I.,	466
Scovil, Sele,	Rec. Conn. Men,	407
	Hist. Waterbury Vol. I.,	466
Smith, David,	Rec. Conn. Men,	116, 142, 360, etc.
	Hist. Waterbury Vol. I.,	466
Smith, Theophilus M.,	Rec. Conn. Men,	653, 663
Southmayd, William,	Rec. Conn. Men,	117, 237, 500, 612
	Hist. Waterbury Vol. I.,	466
Stevens, Henry,	App. for Pension.	
Storrs, Andrew, Rev.,	Rec. Conn. Men,	612
	Hist. Waterbury Vol. I.,	466
Sutliff, Abel,	Rec. Conn. Men,	407
	Hist. Waterbury Vol. I.,	466
Sutliff, John,	Rec. Conn. Men,	501, 612
	Hist. Waterbury Vol. I.,	466
Tomlinson, Victory,	Rec. Conn. Men,	238
Tuttle, Hezekiah,	Rec. Conn. Men,	117, 612
Tuttle, Lemuel,	Rec. Conn. Men,	290, 637, 653
Upson, Ashbel,	D. A. R. Lin. Book Vol. XXVIII.,	121
Upson, Benjamin,	Rec. Conn. Men,	501, 612
Warner, James,	Rec. Conn. Men,	406
	Hist. Waterbury Vol. I.,	466
Warner, John, Jr., Capt.,	Rec. Conn. Men,	575
	D. A. R. Lin. Book Vol. XXVII.,	234
Weed, Jesse,	Rec. Conn. Men,	117
	Hist. Waterbury Vol. I.,	466
Welton, Benjamin,	Rec. Conn. Men,	179, 181, 339
	Hist. Waterbury Vol. I.,	466
Woodin, Abner,	Rec. Conn. Men,	291
	Hist. Waterbury Vol. I.,	467
*Woodworth, William,	D. A. R. Lin. Book Vol. XXIV.,	29
(Served from New York).		
Wright, Joseph Allyn, Maj.,	Rec. Conn. Men,	81, 104, 194, 322, 337, 367, 374, 637

Salisbury

Revolutionary Soldiers

OF

Salisbury

COMPILED BY
MARY FLOYD TALLMADGE CHAPTER
DAUGHTERS OF THE AMERICAN REVOLUTION
LITCHFIELD, CONN.

Revolutionary Soldiers of Salisbury

Name	Authority	Page
Ackley, Champin, Corp.,	Rolls and Lists,	111
	Rec. Conn. Men,	207
	Lists and Returns,	78, 227
Adams, Joshua,	Rec. Conn. Men,	258
Adams, Silas,	Rec. Conn. Men,	583
Allen, Levi,	Rec. Conn. Men,	31
Annable, Abraham,	Rec. Conn. Men,	207
Archible, David,	Rec. Conn. Men,	562
Baker, Ozias,	Lists and Returns,	78, 227
Baker, William, Sergt.,	Rolls and Lists,	83
	Rec. Conn. Men,	261
	Lists and Returns,	227
Barnes, Elijah,	Rec. Conn. Men,	562
Barret, Hildrake,	Rec. Conn. Men,	220
	Lists and Returns,	78, 227
Beattolpts, Hezekiah,	Rec. Conn. Men,	562
Beebe, David, Capt.,	Rec. Conn. Men,	365, 613
Beebe, Peter,	D. A. R. Lin. Book Vol. XXVII.,	122
Bellows, Samuel,	Rec. Conn. Men,	216
Benton, David,	D. A. R. Lin. Book Vol. XIX.,	125
*Bingham, Silas,	D. A. R. Lin. Book Vol. XXVI.,	210
Blodget, Artemas,	Rolls and Lists,	111
	Rec. Conn. Men,	208
	Lists and Returns,	24, 78, 163, 227
Bostwick, Daniel,	Lists and Returns,	79, 227
Bostwick, Salmon,	Gen. Huntington's Note Book.	
	Lists and Returns,	227
	Rec. Conn. Men,	208
Bradley, James, Sergt.,	Rec. Conn. Men,	208
	Lists and Returns,	78, 227
Bradley, Zenas, Sergt.,	Rolls and Lists,	111
Briant, Alexander,	Rec. Conn. Men,	583
Brinsmade, Daniel, 1st Lieut.,	Rec. Conn. Men,	414
Buel, Nathaniel,	D. A. R. Lin. Book Vol. X.,	180
	Rec. Conn. Men,	61
Buel, Nathaniel, Lieut-Col.,	Rec. Conn. Men,	110
Bundy, Elijah H.,	Rec. Conn. Men,	664
Cammell, Daniel, (Campbell)	Lists and Returns,	78
Campbell, Archibald,	Rec. Conn. Men,	664
Chapple, ———,	Rec. Conn. Men,	209
Chapple, Ameziah,	Lists and Returns,	26

Name	Authority	Page
Chappel, Curtis,	Rolls and Lists,	88, 111
	Lists and Returns,	78, 262
Chipman, John, Capt.,	Lists and Returns,	165
Chipman, Nathaniel, Lieut.,	Rec. Conn. Men,	158
Chipman, Thomas,	Lists and Returns,	75, 227, 262
Clanghorn, Eleazar, Lieut.,	Rec. Conn. Men,	110, 206
Capt.,	Rec. Conn. Men,	242
	Lists and Returns,	26, 78, 165
Clemons, Reuben,	Lists and Returns,	227
Cochran, Samuel,	Rec. Conn. Men,	261
Cook, Nathan,	Rec. Conn. Men,	282
	Lists and Returns,	262
Cool, Himan,	Rolls and Lists,	111
	Lists and Returns,	227
Cool, Isaac,	Rolls and Lists,	111
	Rec. Conn. Men,	209, 364
	Lists and Returns,	78, 227
Coon, Jacob,	Lists and Returns,	78
Coon, James, Q't'rmaster,	Rec. Conn. Men,	257
	Lists and Returns,	57, 165, 227
Coon, James, Fifer,	Rec. Conn. Men,	258, 627
(Killed. Perhaps two men of the same name).		
Coon, John,	Rec. Conn. Men,	258
	Lists and Returns,	227
Curtis, Benjamin,	Rec. Conn. Men,	280
	Hist. of Camden, N. Y.,	533
Davison, Benjamin,	Rec. Conn. Men,	261
	Lists and Returns,	227
Dean, Seth,	Rec. Conn. Men,	583
Dory, Nathan, Ensign,	Rec. Conn. Men,	613
Dutcher, Ruloff, Capt.,	Hist. of Sharon,	73
Eldredge, William,	Rolls and Lists,	111
Emerson, ———,	Rec. Conn. Men,	210
	Lists and Returns,	78, 227
Emorson, Nathaniel,	Rolls and Lists,	111
Eno, William,	Rec. Conn. Men,	258, 361, 627
	Lists and Returns,	227
*Everett, Joseph, Corp.,	D. A. R. Lin. Book Vol. XXVI.,	159
Everist, Benjamin,	Rec. Conn. Men,	274
	Lists and Returns,	227
Everts, Daniel, Corp.,	Rec. Conn. Men,	207
	Lists and Returns,	78
Everts, John,	Rec. Conn. Men,	583
Everts, Stephen,	Rolls and Lists,	267
(Evits)	Rec. Conn. Men,	258
	See New Milford List.	
Farnham, Bezaleel,	Rec. Conn. Men,	210
Field, John,	Lists and Returns,	227
Fisk, Samuel,	Gen. Huntington's Note Book.	
	Lists and Returns,	78

SALISBURY 159

Name	Authority	Page
Fitch, Joseph Trumbull,	Rec. Conn. Men,	210
	Lists and Returns,	28, 78, 168, 227
Fitzgerald, Henry,	Rolls and Lists,	111
	Rec. Conn. Men,	210
	Lists and Returns,	28, 78, 227
Forgarson, Daniel,	Lists and Returns,	29, 78
Fraim, John, Corp.,	Rec. Conn. Men,	258
Frisbie, Nathaniel,	Rec. Conn. Men,	562
Frisbie, Whitfield,	Rec. Conn. Men,	583
Fuller, Amos,	Rec. Conn. Men,	562
Fuller, Joseph,	Rec. Conn. Men,	258
Gates, William,	Lists and Returns,	227
Graves, Benjamin,	Rolls and Lists,	111
	Rec. Conn. Men,	211
	Lists and Returns,	78, 227
Green, William,	Rec. Conn. Men,	280
Grenold, Amasy,	Rolls and Lists,	102
(Born in Saybrook).		
Grinnall, Amasa,	Rec. Conn. Men,	211
	Lists and Returns,	78, 227
(Born in Saybrook).		
Grinnol, Amasa, Corp.,	Rolls and Lists,	111
(Born in Saybrook).		
(Above three names probably the same man).		
Griswold, ———,	Rolls and Lists,	111
Griswold, ———,	Rolls and Lists,	111
Griswold, Eber,	Rec. Conn. Men,	261
	Lists and Returns,	227
Griswold, George,	Rec. Conn. Men,	211
	Lists and Returns,	78, 227
Griswold, Samuel,	Rec. Conn. Men,	211, 366
	Lists and Returns,	78, 227
	D. A. R. Lin. Book Vol. XXVII.,	295
Hale, Asahel, Jr.,	D. A. R. Lin. Book Vol. XVII.,	110
Hastings, Ebenezer,	Rec. Conn. Men,	286
Havens, John,	Lists and Returns,	78
Hawley, John, (Holly)	Lists and Returns,	78, 227
Holcomb, Timothy,	Rec. Conn. Men,	61
Holden, Amos,	Pension List.	
Holdridge, ———,	Rec. Conn. Men,	280
Hollista (ter), Joseph,	Rec. Conn. Men,	664
House, Benjamin, (Hows)	Rec. Conn. Men,	275
	Lists and Returns,	227
Hull, Daniel, Corp.,	Rolls and Lists,	111
	Rec. Conn. Men,	211
	Lists and Returns,	78, 227
Hull, Giles, Sergt.,	Rec. Conn. Men,	206
	Lists and Returns,	31, 78, 168, 355
Hull, Henry, Sergt.,	Rolls and Lists,	111
	Rec. Conn. Men,	211
	Lists and Returns,	78, 227

LITCHFIELD COUNTY REVOLUTIONARY SOLDIERS

Name	Authority	Page
Hull, Jonathan, Corp.,	Rolls and Lists,	111
	Rec. Conn. Men,	211
	Lists and Returns,	227
Hull, Moses,	Rec. Conn. Men,	211
	Lists and Returns,	78, 227
Jones, Ethiel,	Rec. Conn. Men,	583
Kelsey, Samuel,	Rolls and Lists,	21
	See Torrington List.	
Landon, Rufus,	Rec. Conn. Men,	664
Larrabee, Willet,	Rolls and Lists,	89
	Lists and Returns,	34, 78
Lee, Noah, Lieut.,	Rec. Conn. Men,	260, 376
	Lists and Returns,	57, 171, 266
Lee, Samuel, Capt.,	D. A. R. Lin. Book Vol. XIX.,	310
Lewis, Thomas,	Lists and Returns,	78
Lord, Elisha,	Rolls and Lists,	52
Manhiel, William,	Rec. Conn. Men,	278
Matthewson, William,	Rec. Conn. Men,	212
	Lists and Returns,	78
McCarter, George, (Prisoner).	Lists and Returns,	227, 267
McIntire, Henry,	Rec. Conn. Men,	366
	Lists and Returns,	57, 80
(A Henry Mackintire given as of Sharon).		
McLean, ———,	Rec. Conn. Men,	207
	Rec. Conn. Men,	364, 365
	Lists and Returns,	78
McLean, Henry,	Rec. Conn. Men,	362
McLean, Jacob, Sergt.,	Rolls and Lists,	110
	Rec. Conn. Men,	365
	Lists and Returns,	35, 78, 227, 267
McLean, John, Sergt.,	Rolls and Lists,	110
	Lists and Returns,	227
Meigs, Simeon,	Rolls and Lists,	111
	Lists and Returns,	78, 227, 267
Meigs, Simon,	Rec. Conn. Men,	212
Montgomery, Hugh,	App. for Pension.	
Moore, Rogers, Lieut.,	Hist. of Sharon,	67, 192
	Rec. Conn. Men,	93, 613
Morgan, Joshua,	Lists and Returns,	355
Munger, Billey,	Rolls and Lists,	111
	Rec. Conn. Men,	212
	Lists and Returns,	35, 78, 227, 267
Noble, James, Sergt.,	Rec. Conn. Men,	583
Owen, Alvin, (alias David Thrall)	Lists and Returns,	36
Owen (s), Asa,	Rolls and Lists,	111
	Lists and Returns,	79, 227
Owen, Eliphalet,	Rec. Conn. Men,	213
	Lists and Returns,	36, 78, 172, 227

SALISBURY

Name	Authority	Page
Owens, David,	Rec. Conn. Men,	275
	Lists and Returns,	227
Painter, Gamaliel, Capt.,	Rec. Conn. Men,	289 (see 290)
	Lists and Returns,	173, 268
Parish, Jacob,	Rec. Conn. Men,	261
	Lists and Returns,	227
Peas, Jesse,	Rec. Conn. Men,	213
Peck, Frederick,	Rec. Conn. Men,	562
Pooles, John,	Rec. Conn. Men,	274
Porter, Joshua, Col.,	D. A. R. Lin. Book Vol. XVII.,	226
	Rec. Conn. Men,	31, 437, 510, 583
Post, Stephen,	Rolls and Lists,	55
Quackenbush, Abraham,	Rec. Conn. Men,	627
Reed, Elias, Jr.,	Rec. Conn. Men,	562
Roberts, William, Fifer,	Rec. Conn. Men,	261
	Lists and Returns,	227
*Russell, James, Sergt.,	D. A. R. Lin Book Vol. XXIII.,	57
Russell, John,	Rec. Conn. Men,	664
Sage, Simeon,	Rec. Conn. Men,	664
Schophel, Benjamin,	Lists and Returns,	79
Scofield, Benjamin,	Rec. Conn. Men,	225
Scovil, Benjamin,	Rec. Conn. Men,	361
	Lists and Returns,	227
Selleck, James,	Rec. Conn. Men,	562
Sellock, Nathaniel,	Rec. Conn. Men,	214
Sheldon, Elisha, Col.,	Rec. Conn. Men,	271, 376
Maj.,	Rec. Conn. Men,	444, 475
	Lists and Returns,	175, 270
Shipman, Thomas,	Rec. Conn. Men,	365
Smith, Elijah,	Rec. Conn. Men,	562
Smith, Isaac,	Rec. Conn. Men,	225
Stoddard, Darius, Surgeon,	Rec. Conn. Men,	363, 627
Stoddard, Josiah,	Rec. Conn. Men,	31, 272
Stoddard, Samuel, Sergt.,	Rec. Conn. Men,	363, 627
	Lists and Returns,	227
Strong, Adonijah, Lieut.,	Rec. Conn. Men,	63, 124, 376
Strong, Phinehas, Corp.,	Rolls and Lists,	111
	Rec. Conn. Men,	214
	Lists and Returns,	79, 175, 227, 270
Strong, Reuben,	Rec. Conn. Men,	627
	Lists and Returns,	40, 79, 227
Surdam, Peter,	Rec. Conn. Men,	225
	Lists and Returns,	227
Sweetland, Aaron,	Rec. Conn. Men,	289
	Lists and Returns,	175, 227, 270
Tarry, Tiam, Sergt.,	Rolls and Lists,	111
Terry, Gamalel, Sergt.,	Rec. Conn. Men,	361
	Lists and Returns,	79, 227
Thompson, Joel,	Rec. Conn. Men,	258
(Prisioner, exchanged).		

Name	Authority	Page
Torrey, Gamaliel, Sergt.,	Rec. Conn. Men,	215
Tousley, Job,	Gen. Huntington's Note Book.	
	Rec. Conn. Men,	215
	Lists and Returns,	79, 227
Tubbs, Martin, Corp.,	Rolls and Lists,	111
	Rec. Conn. Men,	215
	Lists and Returns,	79, 227
Tupper, William, Quartermaster,	Rolls and Lists,	111
	Rec. Conn. Men,	33, 207
	App. for Pension.	
	Lists and Returns,	42, 78, 176, 227
Waterhouse, Samuel,	Rec. Conn. Men,	275
Welch, Micael,	Lists and Returns,	227
Wellden, Isaac,	Lists and Returns,	79, 227
Welldon, Abraham,	App. for Pension.	
	Lists and Returns,	79
White, Laurence,	Rec. Conn. Men,	277
White, William,	Rolls and Lists,	111
	Rec. Conn. Men,	216, 363
	Lists and Returns,	78, 227
Whitney, ———,	Rolls and Lists,	111
(Gen. Huntington's Note Book gives a Solomon Whitney).		
Whitney, Asa, Armourer,	Rec. Conn. Men,	93
Whitney, Solomon,	Rec. Conn. Men,	216
	Lists and Returns,	79, 227
Whitman, George,	Lists and Returns,	227
Wightman, George,	Rec. Conn. Men,	259
Wild, John,	Rec. Conn. Men,	216
	Lists and Returns,	79
Wolcott, Claudy,	Rec. Conn. Men,	562
Woodward, Joseph,	Gen. Huntington's Note Book.	
Woodworth, Ephraim, Capt.,	D. A. R. Lin. Book Vol. XXVIII.,	114
Woodworth, Samuel,	Rec. Conn. Men,	569
Yarno, Johnson,	Rec. Conn. Men,	259
Yates, William,	Rolls and Lists,	111
	Lists and Returns,	44, 79, 177

Sharon

Revolutionary Soldiers

OF

Sharon

COMPILED BY
MARY FLOYD TALLMADGE CHAPTER
DAUGHTERS OF THE AMERICAN REVOLUTION
LITCHFIELD, CONN.

Revolutionary Soldiers of Sharon

Name	Authority	Page
Abel, William,	Hist. Sharon,	113
(Abel, Wm. Robt.)	Rec. Conn. Men,	562
Ackley, Ariel, Musician,	Rec. Conn. Men,	219
	Lists and Returns,	57, 80
Ackley, David,	Hist. Sharon,	190
Ackley, Thomas, Jr.,	Hist. Sharon,	69, 113
Ady, Thomas,	Rec. Conn. Men,	611
Allen, Amos,	Rec. Conn. Men,	194, 639
Allen, Ichabod,	Rec. Conn. Men,	611
	Lists and Returns,	21, 236
Ames, Samuel,	Rec. Conn. Men,	664
Avery, Daniel,	Lists and Returns,	80
Baker, Joseph,	Rec. Conn. Men,	562
Baley, Joseph,	Rec. Conn. Men,	611
Bardslee, John,	Rec. Conn. Men,	611
Barto, John,	Rec. Conn. Men,	276
Beatts, Hezekiah,	Rec. Conn. Men,	583
Bemon, Mathew,	App. for Pension.	
Benjamin, Phineas,	Rec. Conn. Men,	220
	Lists and Returns,	57, 80
Betts, Zephar,	Rec. Conn. Men,	611
	Lists and Returns,	211
Bill, Jude,	Hist. Sharon,	190
	Rec. Conn. Men,	220
	Lists and Returns,	57, 80, 165
Boland, Azariah, Ensign,	Rec. Conn. Men,	613
Boland, David, Cornet,	Hist. Sharon,	73, 117
	Rec. Conn. Men,	611
Boland, William, Capt.,	Hist. Sharon,	69, 117
	Rec. Conn. Men,	613
Botchford, Ephraim,	Rec. Conn. Men,	611
Brackmay, Wotstone,	Rec. Conn. Men,	611
Brackway, Timothy,	Lists and Returns,	57, 80
Briggs, John,	Rec. Conn. Men,	583
Brockway, Asa,	Hist. Sharon,	118
	Rec. Conn. Men,	562
Buel, Eliphalet,	Rec. Conn. Men,	611
Buel, Nathaniel,	Hist. Sharon,	69
Calkin, Abner,	Lists and Returns,	80
	Rec. Conn. Men,	221

168   LITCHFIELD COUNTY REVOLUTIONARY SOLDIERS

Name	Authority	Page
Calkin, Abner, (Colkin)	Lists and Returns,	57
Calkin, Derias,	Lists and Returns,	57, 80
Calkin, Elisha,	Hist. Sharon,	190
Calkin, Jesse,	Hist. Sharon,	190
Calkin, Reuben, Sergt.,	Hist. Sharon,	70, 190
Campbell, Daniel,	Rec. Conn. Men,	276
Campbell, John,	Rec. Conn. Men,	562
Canfield, Samuel, Col.,	Hist. Sharon,	120
	Rec. Conn. Men,	143
(Another from New Milford).		
Carrier, Timothy,	Rec. Conn. Men,	611
*Cartwright, Christopher,	Hist. Sharon,	121
Cartwright, Reuben,	Hist. Sharon,	190
Cartwright, Samuel,	Hist. Sharon,	121
Chaffee, Joel,	Rec. Conn. Men,	664
Chaffee, Joshua,	Rec. Conn. Men,	611
Chamberlain, Isaac, Sergt.,	Hist. Sharon,	122, 190
	Rec. Conn. Men,	293
Chapman, Amos, 1st Lieut.,	Rec. Conn. Men,	60
Chapman, Elias,	Rec. Conn. Men,	611
Chapman, Lemuel,	Rec. Conn. Men,	329
	D. A. R. Lin. Book Vol. XXVII.,	220
Chapman, Nehemiah,	Rec. Conn. Men,	611
Chapman, Robert,	Rec. Conn. Men,	611
Chappel, Amos, Lieut.,	Hist. Sharon,	192
Chasee, Joshua,	Rec. Conn. Men,	562
Clark, Daniel,	Rec. Conn. Men,	664
Clary, Daniel,	Rec. Conn. Men,	277
Clary, Samuel,	Rec. Conn. Men,	281
Cleveland, Josiah, Sergt.,	Rec. Conn. Men,	219
	Lists and Returns,	25, 79, 165, 236
Cluxton, Samuel,	Rec. Conn. Men,	361
	Hist. Sharon,	123
Cole, Mathew,	From Farmington.	
Coleman, Josiah, Jr.,	Hist. Sharon,	69, 123
Crippen, Thomas,	Rec. Conn. Men,	611
Davis, James,	Lists and Returns,	124
Delano, Thomas,	Rec. Conn. Men,	611
Dorman, Gershom,	Rec. Conn. Men,	276
	Lists and Returns,	167, 263
Dotey, David, Capt.,	Hist. Sharon,	69, 127
Dotey, Samuel,	D. A. R. Lin. Book Vol. XIX.,	284
Downs, David, Capt.,	Hist. Sharon,	69, 127
	Rec. Conn. Men,	110
Elmer, Samuel, Col.,	Hist. Sharon,	71, 129, 192
(Elmore)	Rec. Conn. Men,	113
Elmer, Samuel, Jr., Lieut.,	Hist. Sharon,	71, 172
	Rec. Conn. Men,	113

SHARON

Name	Authority	Page
Elmore, Daniel, (Elmer)	Rec. Conn. Men, Lists and Returns,	222 28, 57, 79, 119, 167, 236
Elmore, Daniel, Jr.,	Lists and Returns,	80
Elmore, Elijah,	D. A. R. Lin. Book Vol. XIV.,	210
Everet, John,	Rec Conn. Men,	611
Everett, Ebe,	Hist. Sharon, Rec. Conn. Men, D. A. R. Lin. Book Vol. XXV.,	129, 190 611 141
Everett, Eliphalet,	Hist. Sharon, Rec. Conn. Men, Lists and Returns,	129 222, 299 80
Fairchild, Jessee,	D. A. R. Lin. Book Vol. XIV.,	235
Fisher, Isaac,	Rec. Conn. Men, Lists and Returns,	222 79, 168, 236, 264
Foster, Benjamin,	App. for Pension. Rec. Conn. Men, Lists and Returns,	 222 29, 80, 168, 236
Foster, Elijah 2nd, Lieut.,	Hist. Sharon, Rec. Conn. Men,	69, 130 414
Freeman, Call,	App. Pension.	
Frink, Seth,	Rolls and Lists,	52
Frisbie, Hezekiah, Lieut.,	Hist. Sharon, Rec. Conn. Men, D. A. R. Lin. Book Vol. X.,	69 613 298
Fuller, Amos,	Rec. Conn. Men,	562
Fuller, Benjamin,	Rec. Conn. Men,	611
Fuller, Jehiel,	Rec. Conn. Men,	583
Fuller, John,	Rec. Conn. Men,	664
Fullerton, John,	Rec. Conn. Me·,	664
*Gager, Samuel R., Surgeon,	Hist. Sharon,	131
Gale, William, Trumpeter,	Rec. Conn. Men,	275
Galson, Ebenezer,	Rec. Conn. Men, Lists and Returns,	363 168, 264
Gay, Ebenezer, Lieut.-Col.,	Hist. Sharon, Rec. Conn. Men,	131 437
Gibbs, Sylvanus, Capt.,	Hist. Sharon,	132, 190
Gillet, Charles,	Hist. Sharon,	69, 133
*Gillson, Eleazer,	Hist. Sharon, Lists and Returns,	133 30, 236, 264
Goff, David,	Hist. Sharon, Rec. Conn. Men,	67 93
Goodrich, Charles,	Rec. Conn. Men,	583
Goodrich, David, (Gutrich)	Hist. Sharon, Rec. Conn. Men, Lists and Returns,	70 222 29, 79, 168, 236, 264
Goodrich, Isaac,	D. A. R. Lin. Book Vol. XVII.,	152
Goodrich, John,	Rec. Conn. Men, Lists and Returns,	222 80
Goodrich, Nathan,	Rec. Conn. Men,	329, 362
Goodrich, Solomon,	Hist. Sharon,	190

Name	Authority	Page
Goodrich, William, Corp.,	Hist. Sharon,	190
Goodrich, Zenas,	Hist. Sharon,	190
Goodwin, Hezekiah, Corp.,	Hist. Sharon,	134
	D. A. R. Lin. Book Vol. XVII.,	83
Gray, Daniel, Corp.,	Rec. Conn. Men,	262
Gray, Darius,	Lists and Returns,	57, 80
Gray, James,	D. A. R. Lin. Book Vol. XXVIII.,	167
Gray, John,	Rec. Conn. Men,	93
Gray, Samuel,	Lists and Returns,	57, 80
Gray, William,	Hist. Sharon,	68, 135
Griswold, Adonijah, Capt.,	Hist. Sharon,	69, 136
Griswold, Azariah, Ensign,	Hist. Sharon,	69, 135
Hamilton, David,	Rec. Conn. Men,	275
Hamilton, Joseph,	Rec. Conn. Men,	611
Hamilton, Samuel,	Rec. Conn. Men,	611
Hamlin, Asa,	D. A. R. Lin. Book Vol. XX.,	108
Hamlin, Cornelius,	Rec. Conn. Men,	223
	Lists and Returns,	57, 80
Hamlin, Jones,	Rec. Conn. Men,	583
Hamlin, Nathaniel,	Hist. Sharon,	69
	Rec. Conn. Men,	395
Hatch, John,	Rec. Conn. Men,	664
Hatch, Oliver,	Rec. Conn. Men,	277
Hatch, Timothy,	Rec. Conn. Men,	277
Heath, John,	Rec. Conn. Men,	293
Heath, Thomas,	Hist. Sharon,	66, 190
	Rec. Conn. Men,	664
Hollister, John,	Hist. Sharon,	74, 140, 190
Hoskins, Ira,	Rec. Conn. Men,	256, 627
Hotchkiss, Asahel,	Rec. Conn. Men,	664
Hunt, Phineas,	Rec. Conn. Men,	611
Hunter, Ebenezer,	Rec. Conn. Men,	611
Hunter, Nathaniel,	Hist. Sharon,	141
	Rec. Conn. Men,	664
Hutchinson, Ezra,	Rec. Conn. Men,	611
Ingram, Amaziah,	Lists and Returns,	213
Jackson, Ebenezer,	Rec. Conn. Men,	611
Jackson, Jehiel,	Hist. Sharon,	190
Jackson, John,	D. A. R. Lin. Book Vol. XI.,	356
Jackson, Stephen,	Rec. Conn. Men,	611
Jagun, William,	Rec. Conn. Men,	562
Jennings, Jabez,	Hist Sharon,	69
Jewitt, Alpheus,	Rec. Conn. Men,	664
Jewitt, Caleb, Capt.,	Rec. Conn. Men,	329, 574, 611
Johns, Joel,	Gen. Huntington's Note Book.	
Johnson, George,	Rec. Conn. Men,	562
Johnson, Robert,	Rolls and Lists,	89
	Lists and Returns,	30, 79, 170, 236, 355

SHARON   171

Name	Authority	Page
Juckett, Elijah,	Hist. Sharon,	143
Keeler, Lewis,	Rec. Conn. Men,	329, 363
Keelor, Levi,	Rec. Conn. Men,	583
Kelsey, Noah,	Rolls and Lists,	69
	Rec. Conn. Men,	363
	Lists and Returns,	33, 80, 170, 236, 266
*King, George,	Hist. Sharon,	143
Knap, Jonas,	Lists and Returns,	57, 80
Knapp, James, Corp.,	Rolls and Lists,	69
	Lists and Returns,	57, 80
	Rec. Conn. Men,	363
Lake, Joseph,	Hist. Sharon,	144
Leon, William,	Lists and Returns,	57, 80
Lewis, Ebenezer,	Rec. Conn. Men,	277
Lewis, Jabez,	Rec. Conn. Men,	224, 363
	Lists and Returns,	57, 80
Lewis, Samuel, Jr.,	Hist. Sharon,	67, 145
	Rec. Conn. Men,	93
Lloyd, James,	Rec. Conn. Men,	664
	App. Pension.	
Lord, Joseph, Ensign,	Rec. Conn. Men,	611
Loughlin, James,	Lists and Returns,	57, 80
Lovell, John,	Rec. Conn. Men,	611
	D. A. R. Lin. Book Vol. X.,	93
Luce, Daniel,	Rec. Conn. Men,	611
Mackintire, Henery,	Lists and Returns,	57, 80
Manning, David,	Hist. Sharon,	190
Manning, Thaddeus,	Rec. Conn. Men,	275
Maxam, Adonijah,	Hist. Sharon,	148, 194
	Rec. Conn. Men,	93, 664
McCarthy, George,	Rec. Conn. Men,	259
Menhant, Wheeler,	Rec. Conn. Men,	583
Miller, Gain,	Rec. Conn. Men,	611
Morgan, Nathaniel,	Rec. Conn. Men,	611
Munn, Justus, Corp.,	Rec. Conn. Men,	276
Pangborn, Adonijah,	Lists and Returns,	57, 80
Pardy, James, Lieut.,	Rec. Conn. Men,	583
Park, Ezra,	Rec. Conn. Men,	293
	D. A. R. Lin. Book Vol. XXIII.,	194
Parke, Smith,	Rec. Conn. Men,	611
Parker, Mathew,	Rec. Conn. Men,	611
Parsons, Isaac, (Persons)	Gen. Huntington's Note Book. Lists and Returns,	80
Patchin, Daniel,	Rec. Conn. Men,	276
Perkins, Jason,	App. Pension.	
Pettet, Enoch, (Enos)	Rec. Conn. Men,	362
	Lists and Returns,	37, 79, 172, 236, 268
Pierce, Isaac,	Lists and Returns,	80
Prout, James,	App. Pension.	

Name	Authority	Page
Randall, John, Jr.,	Hist. Sharon,	69
Randolph, David,	Rec. Conn. Men,	279
Ray, Stephen,	Rec. Conn. Men,	611
Rice, Asa,	Rec. Conn. Men,	611
Richard, Nathaniel,	Lists and Returns,	57, 80
Rogers, Asa,	Hist. Sharon,	190
Row, David,	Rec. Conn. Men,	225, 364
	Lists and Returns,	57
Rusco, David, Ensign,	Rec. Conn. Men,	614
Rusco, Jona., (Rust)	Rolls and Lists,	68
	Lists and Returns,	39, 79, 174, 236, 269
Rusco, Peter S.,	Rec. Conn. Men,	276
Rustin, William,	App. Pension.	
Sanders, Joseph,	Rec. Conn. Men,	611
Sanders, Joseph, Jr.,	Rec. Conn. Men,	611
Scott, John,	Rec. Conn. Men,	262
Shattrick, Joseph,	Rec. Conn. Men,	611
Sheldon, Elisha, Col.,	Lists and Returns,	41
Sherwood, Lemuel,	Rec. Conn. Men,	225
	Lists and Returns,	80
Sherwood, Timothy,	Rec. Conn. Men,	562
Slauter, Ephraim,	App. Pension.	
Smith, Cotton Mather,	Hist. Sharon,	68, 160
Smith, Eliphalet, Corp.,	Rec. Conn. Men,	225
	Lists and Returns,	57, 80
Smith, Simeon, Capt.,	Hist. Sharon,	69, 165
Smith, Zebrina,	Rolls and Lists,	67
Somers, Asahel,	Hist. Sharon,	69
Southworth, Samuel,	Rec. Conn. Men,	275
Spencer, Alexander, Jr.,	Hist. Sharon,	69, 167
Steadman, Robert, Lieut.,	Rec. Conn. Men,	611
Stephens, Henry,	Lists and Returns,	57, 80
St. John, Silas,	Rec. Conn. Men,	611
St. John, Timothy,	Rec. Conn. Men,	611
Stone, Robin,	App. Pension.	
Strong, Caleb,	Rec. Conn. Men,	611
Strong, David, Capt.,	Hist. Sharon,	70, 168
	Rec. Conn. Men,	194, 322, 327, 375
	Lists and Returns,	40, 79, 174, 236, 269
Strong, Joseph,	Lists and Returns,	57, 80
Strong, Josiah, Jr.,	Hist. Sharon,	168
	Lists and Returns,	57, 80
Stuart, William,	Rolls and Lists,	69
	Lists and Returns,	57, 80
Swetland, Aaron,	Hist. Sharon,	190
Swetland, Southard,	Hist. Sharon,	190
Tickner, John,	Hist. Sharon,	190
Tobias, Daniel,	Rolls and Lists,	69
	Rec. Conn. Men,	363

SHARON

Name	Authority	Page
Tobias, James,	Gen. Huntington's Note Book. Lists and Returns,	57, 80
Tobias, Jona.,	Rolls and Lists,	68
	Lists and Returns,	57, 80
Tucker, Joseph,	Rec. Conn. Men,	226, 361
	Lists and Returns,	57, 80
Tyler, Nathaniel,	Rolls and Lists,	69
	Lists and Returns,	57, 80
Wainright, Thomas,	Rec. Conn. Men,	226
	Lists and Returns,	43, 79, 176, 236
Wallops, Thomas, (Warrups)	Gen. Huntington's Note Book. See Kent List.	
Warner, Amasa,	Rec. Conn. Men,	226, 363
	Lists and Returns,	57, 80
Wells, Stephen,	Lists and Returns,	57, 79
Whitcomb, Robert, Sergt.,	Rec. Conn. Men,	569
White, Artchelus,	Rec. Conn. Men,	611
White, Consider,	Rec. Conn. Men,	329
Whipel, Nathaniel,	Lists and Returns,	79
White, George,	Rec. Conn. Men,	611
White, Solomon,	Rec. Conn. Men,	562
Whitney, Ezekiel,	Rolls and Lists,	69
	Lists and Returns,	57, 80
Wilcox, Barns,	Rec. Conn. Men,	276
Williamson, Zelophehead,	Lists and Returns,	57, 80
*Wilson, John, Capt.,	Rec. Conn. Men,	664
	Hist. Sharon,	171
Wood, Barnabas,	Rec. Conn. Men,	611
Wood, Davis,	Hist. Sharon,	69, 172
Yale, Waitstill,	App. for Pension.	
	Lists and Returns,	44, 79, 177, 236
Young, Lemuel,	Rec. Conn. Men,	611
Youngs, Benjamin,	App. for Pension.	

Torrington

Revolutionary Soldiers

OF

Torrington

COMPILED BY
MARANA NORTON BROOKS CHAPTER
DAUGHTERS OF THE AMERICAN REVOLUTION
TORRINGTON, CONN.

For fuller accounts of these men see original lists

Revolutionary Soldiers of Torrington

Name	Authority	Page
Abbot, Pardon,	Rec. Conn. Men,	632
	Hist. Torrington,	236
Abrow, Bennajah,	Lists and Returns,	59
Apley, Josiah,	Lists and Returns,	205
Atwater, Asaph A.,	Rolls and Lists,	273
	Hist. Torrington,	642
†Austin, Enos,	Hist. Torrington,	223
Bancroft, Oliver,	Rec. Conn. Men,	481, 503, 650
	Hist. Torrington,	645
Barber, Benjamin,	Rolls and Lists,	20, 36
	Rec. Conn. Men,	505, 588
Barber, Elijah,	Hist. Torrington,	646
	Rec. Conn. Men,	87, 562
Barber, Nathaniel,	Hist. Torrington,	646
	Rec. Conn. Men,	220
	Rolls and Lists,	273
	Lists and Returns,	22, 235
Barber, Nathaniel, Jr.,	Hist. Torrington,	230, 646
Barber, Simeon,	Rolls and Lists,	20
	Rec. Conn. Men,	652
Barber, Timothy,	Hist. Torrington,	646
	Rec. Conn. Men,	612, 654
Benedict, Bushnell,	Hist. Torrington,	236
†Benedict, Daniel,	Hist. Torrington,	236
	Rec. Conn. Men,	276, 416, 423
	Lists and Returns,	59
Benedict, Levi,	Rec. Conn. Men,	282, 541, 641
	Lists and Returns,	284
Benham, Isaac,	Lists and Returns,	206
Bigelow, Frederick,	Rec. Conn. Men,	50, 203
	Rolls and Lists,	273
	Lists and Returns,	203
(Torringford).		
Birge, John,	Hist. Torrington,	650
	Rolls and Lists,	273
	Rec. Conn. Men,	549, 652
Birge, Simeon,	Hist. Torrington,	651, 236
Bissell, Ebenezer,	Hist. Torrington,	653
	Rolls and Lists,	273
Bissell, Elijah,	Hist. Torrington,	236, 228
	Rec. Conn. Men,	83, 203, 541
	Lists and Returns,	203
(Torringford).		

Name	Authority	Page
Bissell, Return,	Rolls and Lists,	273
	Rec. Conn. Men,	503, 652
Blake, Elijah,	Rec. Conn. Men,	583, 652
Bosher, Nicholas,	Lists and Returns,	287
Buell, Jesse,	Hist. Torrington,	226
	Rec. Conn. Men,	424
Burr, John,	Rolls and Lists,	273
	Rec. Conn. Men,	541
Burr, Simeon,	Rec. Conn. Men,	583
Camp, John,	Lists and Returns,	59
Carr, Clement,	Hist. Torrington,	666
	Rec. Conn. Men,	640
Catlin, Thomas,	Rec. Conn. Men,	40, 552
	Rolls and Lists,	20
Coe, Oliver,	Hist. Torrington,	669
	See also Winchester List.	
Coe, Oliver, Jr.,	Hist. Torrington,	670
	Rec. Conn. Men,	165
	See also Winchester List.	
Coe, Seth,	Hist. Torrington,	674
	Rec. Conn. Men,	273, 541, 653
Cook, Jesse,	Rolls and Lists,	21
	Rec. Conn. Men,	83, 375, 419
Cook, John,	Hist. Torrington,	222
	D. A. R. Lin. Book Vol. XXVIII.,	246
Curtis, John,	Hist. Torrington,	681
	Rolls and Lists,	39
	Rec. Conn. Men,	221, 612
Day, Isaac,	Rec. Conn. Men,	157
Drake, Noah,	Hist. Torrington,	683
	Rec. Conn. Men,	511, 663
Eggleston, Joseph,	Hist. Torrington,	686
	Rolls and Lists,	60
	Rec. Conn. Men,	583
Ellsworth, John,	Hist. Torrington,	228
	Lists and Returns,	180
Ely, Andrew,	Rec. Conn. Men,	191
	Hist. Torrington,	228
Fay, Timothy,	Lists and Returns,	59
Farmer, Daniel,	Lists and Returns,	59
Ferter, Andrew,	Lists and Returns,	287
Filley, Isaac,	Rolls and Lists,	273
Filley, Remembrance,	Lists and Returns,	59
Frisbie, Benjamin,	Rec. Conn. Men,	63
	Rolls and Lists,	273
	Lists and Returns,	28, 235
Fyler, Ambrose,	Hist. Torrington,	230, 699
	Rolls and Lists,	236
	Lists and Returns,	59
Fyler, John,	Lists and Returns,	206

TORRINGTON 181

Name	Authority	Page
*Fyler, Stephen,	Hist. Torrington,	446
	Rec. Conn. Men,	653
Flowers, Ithurel,	Lists and Returns,	59
Gaylord, Benjamin,	Hist. Torrington,	228
	Rolls and Lists,	21, 36, 119
	Rec. Conn. Men,	203
	Lists and Returns,	30, 235
Gillett, Jabez,	Hist. Torrington,	235, 701
Goodwin, Charles,	Hist. Torrington,	225
	Rolls and Lists,	142
Gleson, Andrew,	Lists and Returns,	202
Gridley, Isaiah,	Rec. Conn. Men,	329
Griswold, Shubael,	Hist. Torrington,	708
	Rec. Conn. Men,	61, 424, 549
Griswold, Shubael, Jr.,	Hist. Torrington,	236, 708
	Rec. Conn. Men,	549
Griswold, Stanley,	Hist. Torrington,	228, 469
Griswold, White,	Rec. Conn. Men,	234
Hills, Belah,	Lists and Returns,	205
Hodges, Elkanah,	Hist. Torrington,	235, 447
Holmes, David,	Rec. Conn. Men,	329
Hoskins, Joseph, Sr.,	Hist. Torrington,	722
	See also Winchester List.	
Hough, Eliphalet,	Hist. Torrington,	228
Hutchen, Jeremiah,	Lists and Returns,	286
Jarols, Amos,	Lists and Returns,	59
Johnson, Jacob,	Rec. Conn. Men,	223, 612
Jones, Samuell,	Lists and Returns,	59
Keley, Samuel, Jr.,	Hist. Torrington,	230
	Lists and Returns,	59
Kelsey, Elisha,	Rolls and Lists,	273
	Rec. Conn. Men,	551
	Hist. Torrington,	228
Kelsey, Nathaniel, Jr.,	Hist. Torrington,	228
Kelsey, Samuel,	Rolls and Lists,	37
	Hist. Torrington,	228
Kelsey, Timothy,	Rolls and Lists,	273
Leach, Ebenezer,	Rec. Conn. Men,	114, 261
	Hist. Torrington,	228, 230
	Lists and Returns,	59
Leach, Richard,	Hist. Torrington,	236, 729
Loomis, Asa,	Hist. Torrington,	736
	Rolls and Lists,	160
	Rec. Conn. Men,	562
Loomis, Brigadier,	Rec. Conn. Men,	203, 235, 283, 503, 541
	Rolls and Lists,	202
	Lists and Returns,	280
†Loomis, Elijah,	Hist. Torrington,	736
	Rolls and Lists,	27
	Rec. Conn. Men,	42, 88

Name	Authority	Page
Loomis, Epaphras,	Hist. Torrington,	735
	Rec. Conn. Men,	396
	Rolls and Lists,	210
Loomis, Epaphras, Jr.,	Hist. Torrington,	225, 735
	Rec. Conn. Men,	612
†Loomis, Remembrance,	Hist. Torrington,	225, 735
	Rec. Conn. Men,	423
Loomis, Timothy,	Hist. Torrington,	737
	Rolls and Lists,	273
	Rec. Conn. Men,	529
Loomis, Wait,	Hist. Torrington,	225, 236, 735
Lyman, David,	Hist. Torrington,	235
	Rec. Conn. Men,	442
Marshall, Almarin,	Rec. Conn. Men,	570
Marshall, Noah,	Rec. Conn. Men,	612
Marshall, Roger,	Hist. Torrington,	228
Mason, Jonathan,	Hist. Torrington,	226
	Rec. Conn. Men,	424
†Mather, Cotton,	Rolls and Lists,	273
	Rec. Conn. Men,	422, 482
Matthews, Thomas,	Rolls and Lists,	273
	Rec. Conn. Men,	541
Merrels, Aaron,	Lists and Returns,	59
Miller, Ebenezer, Lieut.,	Rec. Conn. Men,	502, 531, 565, 614, 653, 663
Miller, Jonathan,	Hist. Torrington,	741
	Rec. Conn. Men,	176
	Rolls and Lists,	203, 273
Moore, Barber,	Hist. Torrington,	228
Newell, Rivaous,	Lists and Returns,	59
North, Phineas,	Hist. Torrington,	750
	Rec. Conn. Men,	562
Nottingham, George,	Lists and Returns,	59
Olmstead, Gemaliel,	Lists and Returns,	59
Osburn, Timothy,	Hist. Torrington,	752
	Rec. Conn. Men,	612
Palmer, Jared,	Hist. Torrington,	229
	Rec. Conn. Men,	583
Ray, Timothy,	Rec. Conn. Men,	329
	Lists and Returns,	205
Reed, Justus,	D. A. R. Lin. Book Vol. XXIV.,	239
Roberts, Abel,	Hist. Torrington,	758
Roberts, Charles,	Rolls and Lists,	273
Roberts, Clerk,	Hist. Torrington,	236
	Lists and Returns,	59
Roberts, Samuel,	Hist. Torrington,	228, 758
	Rolls and Lists,	101
	Rec. Conn. Men,	166, 214, 225
	See also Winchester List.	
Rockwell, John,	Rolls and Lists,	68
	Rec. Conn. Men,	61, 200, 644
Rossiter, Stephen,	Rolls and Lists,	273

TORRINGTON 183

Name	Authority	Page
Rowley, Stephen,	Hist. Torrington,	236
	Rolls and Lists,	47, 145
Scoville, Ebenezer,	Hist. Torrington,	230
	Rolls and Lists,	139
	Rec. Conn. Men,	201
	Lists and Returns,	59
Sheldon, Epaphras,	Hist. Torrington,	225, 762
	Rolls and Lists,	164, 202, 203
Skinner, Thomas,	Rolls and Lists,	273
Smith, Ebenezer,	Hist. Torrington,	764
	Rolls and Lists,	170, 202, 211, 224, 225
	Rec. Conn. Men,	574
Stancliff, John,	Hist. Torrington,	228
	Rec. Conn. Men,	201
Stancliff, Lemuel,	Lists and Returns,	278, 287
Stannard, Seth,	Lists and Returns,	59
Strong, John, Capt., (Col.)	Hist. Torrington,	768
	Rolls and Lists,	224, 225
Sweet, Peleg,	Lists and Returns,	205
Taylor, Joseph,	Rec. Conn. Men,	562
	D. A. R. Lin. Book Vol. XXVII.,	246
Thrall, Levi,	D. A. R. Lin. Book Vol. XXV.,	10
Towee, Joseph,	Lists and Returns,	59
Warner, Asahel,	Rec. Conn. Men,	329
Watson, John,	Rolls and Lists,	227
(Warson)	Rec. Conn. Men,	282, 649
	Lists and Returns,	288
Watson, Levi,	Rec. Conn. Men,	238, 653
	Hist. Torrington,	235
Watson, Thomas,	Hist. Torrington,	774
	Rolls and Lists,	95, 117, 127
	Rec. Conn. Men,	164, 239, 277, 349
Weaver, Coonrod,	Lists and Returns,	59
White, Daniel,	Rec. Conn. Men,	570, 629, 657
White, John,	Lists and Returns,	59
Whiting, Benjamin,	Hist. Torrington,	229, 779
	Rec. Conn. Men,	583
Whiting, Henry,	Hist. Torrington,	236
	Rec. Conn. Men,	68
Whiting, Jesse,	Hist. Torrington,	228, 236
	Rec. Conn. Men,	506
Williams, John,	Hist. Torrington,	236, 786
Williams, William,	Hist. Torrington,	236
Wilson, Amos,	Hist. Torrington,	621
	Rec. Conn. Men,	396
	Rolls and Lists,	139
Wilson, Noah,	Hist. Torrington,	186, 235
	Rec. Conn. Men,	562
Winchell, Daniel,	Rolls and Lists,	273

184 LITCHFIELD COUNTY REVOLUTIONARY SOLDIERS

Name	Authority	Page
Winchell, John,	Rolls and Lists,	67
	Rec. Conn. Men,	653
Woodward, Samuel,	Rec. Conn. Men,	238

From Original Papers given by Mr. Wallace K. Curtiss, of Torrington, formerly of Warren.

Name	Authority	Page
Avery, Thomas, Sergt.,	Rec. Conn. Men,	466, 539
Barnum, Zenas,	Rec. Conn. Men,	35, 196, 228
Beebe, Daniel,	Rec. Conn. Men,	539
Beeman, Truman,	Rec. Conn. Men,	227, 539
Berry, Barnabus,	Rec. Conn. Men,	539
Berry, Cyrus,	Rec. Conn. Men,	539
Berry, John, Corp.,	Rec. Conn. Men,	539
Burnham, Amos,	Not given in Records.	
Carter, Jirah,	Rec. Conn. Men,	328, 352
Case, Aaron,	Rec. Conn. Men,	539
Chamberlain, Bartlett,	Rec. Conn. Men,	539
Chamberlain, Peleg,	Rec. Conn. Men,	466
Cheeney, Richard, (China)	Rec. Conn. Men,	539
(Unless these two are identical, it is a new name).		
Comstock, Abel,	Not given in Records.	
Comstock, Heman,	Not given in Records.	
Curtiss, Augustine,	Rec. Conn. Men,	633, 653
Finney, John,	Rec. Conn. Men,	219
Fowler, Benjamin, Sergt.,	Rec. Conn. Men,	539
Fuller, Abel,	Rec. Conn. Men,	539
Geer, John,	Rec. Conn. Men,	539
Hines, Peter,	Rec. Conn. Men,	539
Ingersoll, Joel,	Rec. Conn. Men,	203
Lyon, Ebenezer,	Rec. Conn. Men,	539
Mallery, Nathaniel,	Rec. Conn. Men,	40
Mills, Lewis, Lieut.,	Rec. Conn. Men,	466, 492, 539
Parrish, Oliver,	Rec. Conn. Men,	539
Peck, Abel,	Rec. Conn. Men,	539
Rust, Levi,	Rec. Conn. Men,	539
Sackett, Alexander,	Rec. Conn. Men,	467, 539
Sackett, Benjamin, Sergt.,	Rec. Conn. Men,	539, 653, 664
Spooner, Nathaniel,	Rec. Conn. Men,	539
Sturtevant, Perez,	Rec. Conn. Men,	539
Tanner, William,	Rec. Conn. Men,	539, 658
Valentine, Gabriel,	Not given in Records.	
Wooster, Jabez, Lieut.,	Not given in Records.	

Washington

Revolutionary Soldiers

BURIED IN

Washington

COMPILED BY
JUDEA CHAPTER
DAUGHTERS OF THE AMERICAN REVOLUTION
WASHINGTON, CONN.

Washington was a part of Woodbury until 1779

Revolutionary Soldiers Buried in Washington

Applicants for Pensions from Washington:

Clark, John 3rd,
Crane, Nathaniel,
Fenn, David,
Guthrie, James,
Hall, John,

Hamlin, Cornelius. Perhaps served from Sharon.
Hull, John,
Northrop, Elijah,
Platt, John,
Trowbridge, Elihu,

Name	Authority	Page
Ackley, Hezekiah,		
Armstrong, James,	Woodbury List.	
Averill, Perry,	Hist. of Woodbury,	485
Baldwin, Enos,	Hist. of Woodbury,	779
Baldwin, Judah,	Hist. of Woodbury,	779
Baker, Jesse, Jr.,	Hist. of Woodbury,	503
Bayard, Marshall,	Lists and Returns,	287
Brinsmade, Daniel N.,	Woodbury List.	
Bryan, Richard,		
Bunce, Isaiah,	Lists and Returns,	163, 236
Bunce, Josiah,	Woodbury List.	
Beeman, Friend,	Lists and Returns,	24, 236
Camp, Isaac,		
Calhoun, John, Dr.,		
Cogswell, William, Maj.,	Woodbury List.	
Davinson, John,	Lists and Returns,	27, 236, 263
Davinson, Isaac, Sergt.,	Lists and Returns,	263
Doane, Ephraim,	Lists and Returns,	287
Farrand, Jonathan,	Lists and Returns, Woodbury List.	236
Fenn, Daniel,	Lists and Returns,	29, 236, 263
Goodsell, Isaac,	Lists and Returns,	210
Hazen, Elijah,	Woodbury List.	
Hickox, Elijah,	Woodbury List.	
Hickox, Nathaniel,	Woodbury List.	
Hine, Jonathan,	Woodbury List.	
Hollister, Gideon, Capt.,	Cothren's Hist.,	586
Hurd, Solomon,	Woodbury List.	
Jordan, John,	Lists and Returns,	33, 236
Judson, David, Capt.,	Rolls and Lists,	76
Leavitt, Samuel,	Woodbury List.	

Name	Authority	Page
Lement, William,	Lists and Returns,	287
Liberty, Jeff,	Woodbury List.	
Marchant, John,	Lists and Returns,	267
Mitchell, Simeon,	Woodbury List.	
Moseley, Abner,	Woodbury List.	
Newton, Ezekiel,	Woodbury List.	
	Lists and Returns,	36, 172, 236
Olds, Oliver,	Woodbury List.	
	Lists and Returns,	36, 172, 236, 267
Parker, Thomas,	Woodbury List.	
Platt, John,	Woodbury List.	
Powel, John, Capt.,		
Rose, Simeon,	Lists and Returns,	287
Taylor, Justus,	Lists and Returns,	287
Thorp, Peter,		
Titus, Joseph,	Rec. Conn. Men,	664
Walker, David,	Woodbury List.	
Whittlesey, David,	Woodbury List.	
Whittlesey, Martin,	Woodbury List.	
Welch, Michael,	Lists and Returns,	23, 44
Welch, Ebenezer,	Lists and Returns,	271

Watertown

Revolutionary Soldiers

OF

Watertown

COMPILED BY
SARAH WHITMAN TRUMBULL CHAPTER
DAUGHTERS OF THE AMERICAN REVOLUTION

Revolutionary Soldiers of Watertown

Name	Authority	Page
Alcox, Solomon,	Rec. Conn. Men,	582
Bachelor, Abel,	Rec. Conn. Men,	208
Baldwin, Theophilus,	Rec. Conn. Men,	221
Barnes, John,	Rec. Conn. Men,	294
Bassett, William,	Rec. Conn. Men,	159
	Lists and Returns,	163, 261
Bartholomew, Saul,	Rec. Conn. Men,	582
Bell, David,	Rec. Conn. Men,	582
Blakeley, Obed, Sergt.,	Rec. Conn. Men,	290
Bradley, Abner,	Rec. Conn. Men,	615, 667
Bradley, Aner, Col.,	Rec. Conn. Men,	492
Bronson, Abel,	Rec. Conn. Men,	615
Bryan, Benajah,	Rec. Conn. Men,	652
Buckingham, David,	History of Waterbury,	429
Cartwright, Thomas,	Rec. Conn. Men,	294
Cole, Thomas,	History of Waterbury,	388
	Rec. Conn. Men,	667
Cook, Arba,	Rec. Conn. Men,	290
Cook, Samuel,	Rec. Conn. Men,	282
Cook, Selah,	Rec. Conn. Men,	281
Curtis, Eli, Lieut.,	Rec. Conn. Men,	230
Curtis, Zara,	Rec. Conn. Men,	281
Curtiss, Enoch,	App. for Pension.	
Cutler, Younglove,	History of Waterbury,	429, 462
Daton, Isaac,	Rec. Conn. Men,	582
Davis, Jonathan,	App. for Pension.	
	Lists and Returns,	166, 263
Dayton, Michael, Capt.,	Rec. Conn. Men,	500
Dayton, Samuel,	History of Waterbury,	462
Dunbar, Joseph,	Rec. Conn. Men,	615
Dutton, Titus, Lieut.,	Rec. Conn. Men,	294
	Lists and Returns,	166
Edwards, Isaac,	History of Waterbury,	568
	D. A. R. Lin. Book Vol. XX.,	116
Edwards, Nathaniel, Capt.,	History of Waterbury,	586
	Lists and Returns,	167, 355
Elton, John, Dr.,	History of Waterbury,	439, 462
Fancher, Jarner,	Rec. Conn. Men,	568
Fenn, Thomas, Capt.,	History of Waterbury,	462
Finch, Jeremiah, (Deserted).	Rec. Conn. Men,	582

LITCHFIELD COUNTY REVOLUTIONARY SOLDIERS

Name	Authority	Page
*Foot, Daniel, (Served in Vermont).	D. A. R. Lin. Book Vol. XXIV.,	291
Fulford, James,	Rec. Conn. Men,	279
	Lists and Returns,	280
Fulford, John, Sergt.,	Rec. Conn. Men,	667
	Lists and Returns,	167, 263
Glazer, John,	Rec. Conn. Men,	348
Grannis, Levi,	Rec. Conn. Men,	582
Grannis, Enos, Lieut.,	History of Waterbury,	463
Guernsey, Jonathan,	History of Waterbury,	463
Guernsey, Joseph, Capt.,	History of Waterbury,	463
(Was one of the guards at Andre's execution).		
Hannon, John,	Rec. Conn. Men,	294
Harmon, John,	Rec. Conn. Men,	294
Heacock, Gideon,	Rec. Conn. Men,	568
Hine, Hezekiah,	D. A. R. Lin. Book Vol. XX.,	302
Hodely, Jude,	Rec. Conn. Men,	294
Hodge, David,	App. for Pension.	
Hummyston, Jared, (Deserted).	Rec. Conn. Men,	280
Hungerford, Stephen,	Rec. Conn. Men,	476
Judd, Alexander,	Rec. Conn. Men,	155
Judd, Joel,	Rec. Conn. Men,	631
Judd, John,	Rec. Conn. Men,	277
Judd, Samuel,	Rec. Conn. Men,	568
Judd, William,	Rec. Conn. Men,	568
Mann, Timothy,	Rec. Conn. Men,	294
Mattoon, Amasa,	Rec. Conn. Men,	500
Mayor, John,	Rec. Conn. Men,	294
Memson, Heman,	Rec. Conn. Men,	236
Merchant, John,	Rec. Conn. Men,	294
Merriam, Christopher,	Rec. Conn. Men,	166
Merriman, Chas., Dr'm Maj.,	History of Waterbury,	464
Merriman, Isaac, Capt.,	History of Waterbury,	464
Parker, Phineas,	Rec. Conn. Men,	617
Pond, Beriah, Artificer,	Rec. Conn. Men,	117, 290
Punderson, David,	Rec. Conn. Men,	568
Ransom, Nicholas,	History of Waterbury,	465
Rice, Nehimiah, Capt.,	Lists and Returns,	268
	Rec. Conn. Men,	375
Seymour, Josiah, Capt.,	History of Waterbury,	466
Smith, David,	Rec. Conn. Men,	373
	Lists and Returns,	174, 269
(Aide-de-camp to the commander-in-chief of the Society of the Cincinnati).		
Steele, Elijah,	Rec. Conn. Men,	324
Stoddard, John, Ensign,	History of Waterbury,	466
	D. A. R. Lin. Book Vol. XX.,	142
Stoddard, Wells,	Rec. Conn. Men,	653
Strickland, David, Sergt.,	Rec. Conn Men,	646

Name	Authority	Page
Trumbull, William,	Rec. Conn. Men,	41
Wade, Increase,	Rec. Conn. Men,	568
Walbridge, George, (Deserted).	Rec. Conn. Men,	294
Warren, Edward,	History of Waterbury,	466
Welton, Samuel,	Rec. Conn. Men,	500
	History of Waterbury,	303, 467
Welton, Shubel,	Rec. Conn. Men,	364
	Lists and Returns,	280
Whitney, John,	Rec. Conn. Men,	277
	History of Waterbury,	467
	Lists and Returns,	280
Williams, Durel,	Rec. Conn. Men,	582
Woodruff, John,	Rec. Conn. Men,	502
	D. A. R. Lin. Book Vol. XX.,	262
Woodruff, Samuel,	Rec. Conn. Men,	476
Woodward, Abel, Capt.,	History of Waterbury,	388, 413
	Rec. Conn. Men,	76

Supplementary List.

Name	Authority	Page
Andrus, Timo.,	Lists and Returns,	163
Camp, Samuel,	Lists and Returns,	166
Cook, Lemuel,	Lists and Returns,	280
Cook, Zarah,	Lists and Returns,	280
Dunbar, Miles,	Lists and Returns,	166, 355
Gaylord, Jonathan,	Lists and Returns,	264, 280
Hecox, E.,	Lists and Returns,	168
Judd, Brewster,	Lists and Returns,	170
Livingston, Isaac,	Lists and Returns,	280
Parker, Isaac,	Lists and Returns,	173, 268
Pendleton, Daniel, Capt.,	Lists and Returns,	173, 268
Preston, A.,	Lists and Returns,	173
Smith, John, (Deserted).	Lists and Returns,	269, 355
Williams, Obidiah,	Lists and Returns,	177

Names of Revolutionary Soldiers whose graves have been located in Watertown:

Baldwin, Theophilus, Ens'n,
Bradley, Aner, Col.,
Bryan, Benajah,
Buckingham, David,
Bronson, Abel,

Cole, Thomas,
Dayton, Michael, Capt.,
Hickox, Isaiah,
Mattoon, Amasa,
Merriam, Christopher,

Cutler, Younglove,
Dayton, Samuel,
Elton, John, Dr.,
Garnsey, Joseph, Capt.,
Guernsey, Jonathan,
Loveland, Ashbel,
Merriman, Charles, Drum
    Maj.,
Merriman, Isaac, Capt.,
Munson, Heman,

Seymour, Joash,
Seymour, Josiah, Capt.,
Steele, Elijah,
Stoddard, John, Ensign,
Stoddard, Wells,
Trumbull, William,
Warren, Edward,
Woodruff, John, Capt.,
Woodruff, Samuel,
Woodward, Abel, Capt.,

Winchester

Revolutionary Soldiers

OF

Winchester

COMPILED BY
GREEN WOODS CHAPTER
DAUGHTERS OF THE AMERICAN REVOLUTION
WINSTED, CONN.

For fuller accounts of these men see original lists

Revolutionary Soldiers of Winchester

Name	Authority	Page
Abro, Benajah,	Rolls and Lists,	36
	Rec. Conn. Men,	185, 319, 632
	Boyd's Annals,	149
Adkins, Josiah, (Atkins)	Rec. Conn. Men,	43
	Boyd's Annals,	162
Alderman, Epaph,	Lists and Returns,	144
(Hired by Garstum Fay).		
Alvord, Eliphas,	Boyd's Annals,	63
Andrews, Abraham or	Rec. Conn. Men,	518
Abram,	Boyd's Annals,	105
Andrews, Daniel,	Rec. Conn. Men,	165
	Boyd's Annals,	106
Arnold, John,	Boyd's Annals,	162
Arnold, Stephen,	Rec. Conn. Men,	62
	Boyd's Annals,	161
Austin, David,	Rec. Conn. Men,	612
	Boyd's Annals,	43, 163
	D. A. R. Lin. Book Vol. XXVII.,	38
Balcom, John,	Boyd's Annals,	29, 162, 346
Balcom, John, Jr.,	Boyd's Annals,	163, 266
Balcom, Jonathan,	Rec. Conn. Men,	583
	Boyd's Annals,	266
Balcom, Nathan,	Boyd's Annals,	161, 267
Balcom, Nathaniel,	Rec. Conn. Men,	62, 63
	Boyd's Annals,	266
	Rolls and Lists,	39
Balcom, Elias,	Boyd's Annals,	267
*Beckley, Richard,	Rec. Conn. Men,	664
Beebe, David,	Boyd's Annals,	162, 196
Benedict, Timothy,	Boyd's Annals,	163
Blackman, Nathan,	Rolls and Lists,	39, 78
	Boyd's Annals,	162
	Rec. Conn. Men,	69
*Blackman, Peter,	Boyd's Annals,	131
*Blake, Elijah,	Rec. Conn. Men,	583, 652
	Boyd's Annals,	208
	D. A. R. Lin. Book Vol. XXVIII.,	172
Brewster, John,	Rolls and Lists,	131
	Rec. Conn. Men,	632
Brownson, Benoni,	Rec. Conn. Men,	49
	Boyd's Annals,	154, 162
Brownson, Ozias,	Rec. Conn. Men,	502
	Boyd's Annals,	109

Litchfield County Revolutionary Soldiers

Name	Authority	Page
*Burr, Jehiel,	Rec. Conn. Men,	503
	Rolls and Lists,	35
	Boyd's Annals,	325
Castle, Elijah, (Castel)	Rec. Conn. Men,	502
	Boyd's Annals,	120
Castle, William,	Rec. Conn. Men,	502
Catlin, Roswell,	Lists and Returns,	213
*Chase, Jedediah,	Rec. Conn. Men,	653
*Church, John,	Rec. Conn. Men,	253, 613
	Boyd's Annals,	144
Clark, Samuel,	Rec. Conn. Men,	562
	Boyd's Annals,	131
*Cleveland, Rufus,	See Barkhamsted List.	
(Served from Ellington).		
Coe, Ebenezer,	Boyd's Annals,	161
Coe, Jonathan,	Rolls and Lists,	222
	Boyd's Annals,	52, 129
Coe, Oliver,	Boyd's Annals,	51
	Lists and Returns,	189
Coe, Oliver, Jr.,	Rec. Conn. Men,	165
	Boyd's Annals,	53
Coit, Richard,	Rec. Conn. Men,	502
	Boyd's Annals,	148, 163
	Lists and Returns,	281
Cone, Daniel Hurlbut,	Rec. Conn. Men,	47, 653
	Rolls and Lists,	135
	Boyd's Annals,	150
*Cook, Shubael,	Boyd's Annals,	503
Corbin, Daniel,	Rec. Conn. Men,	612
	Boyd's Annals,	163, 174
Corbin, Peter,	Boyd's Annals,	162
	Lists and Returns,	213
Corbin, Peter, Jr.,	Rec. Conn. Men,	583, 625
*Dear, John, Jr., (Dare)	Boyd's Annals,	151
*Dear, Jonathan,	Rec. Conn. Men,	365
	Boyd's Annals,	151
Derby, John,	Boyd's Annals,	275
Dolphin, Richard,	Boyd's Annals,	147
Everitt, Andrew,	Rec. Conn. Men,	612
	Boyd's Annals,	50
Everitt, Josiah, Dr.,	Boyd's Annals,	50
Everitt, Noble, Rev.,	Boyd's Annals,	49
Fay, John,	Rec. Conn. Men,	173, 249
	Lists and Returns,	84
Fay, Gershom,	Rec. Conn. Men,	173, 249
	Boyd's Annals,	162
	Lists and Returns,	29, 61, 84, 168
Fay, Timothy,	Rec. Conn. Men,	173, 249
	Boyd's Annals,	162
	Lists and Returns,	29, 60, 84, 168

Name	Authority	Page
Fay, William,	Rec. Conn. Men,	173, 249
	Boyd's Annals,	162
	Lists and Returns,	29, 60, 84, 168
Filley, Abraham,	Boyd's Annals,	40
Filley, Remembrance,	Rec. Conn. Men,	249, 353
	Rolls and Lists,	122
	Boyd's Annals,	163
	Lists and Returns,	61, 84, 168
*Fyler, John, (Filer)	Rec. Conn. Men,	198
Gibbs, Darius,	Rolls and Lists,	39
Gibbs, Truman,	Rec. Conn. Men,	40
	Boyd's Annals,	162
Gibbs, Warham,	Rec. Conn. Men,	61, 424
	Rolls and Lists,	211
	Boyd's Annals,	65
*Gleason, Noah,	Rec. Conn. Men,	63
	Boyd's Annals,	161
	Rolls and Lists,	203
*Goff, David,	Hist. of Sharon,	67
*Goff, Comfort,	Rec. Conn. Men,	108, 174
	Boyd's Annals,	286
Grant, Roswell,	Rec. Conn. Men,	228, 653
	Boyd's Annals,	176
*Grinnell, Michael,		
Griswold, Phineas,	Boyd's Annals,	112
Griswold, Felix,	Lists and Returns,	213
*Hatch, Moses, Capt.,	Rec. Conn. Men,	249, 331, 434
	Boyd's Annals,	191
	D. A. R. Lin. Book Vol. XXVII.,	244
Hills, Bela,	Rolls and Lists,	67
Hills, John,	Boyd's Annals,	45, 164
Hills, Seth,	Boyd's Annals,	44, 163
Hills, Zimri,	Rec. Conn. Men,	583
	Boyd's Annals,	45
*Holmes, David,	Boyd's Annals,	298
*Holmes, Joseph,	Rec. Conn. Men,	503
	Hist. Torrington,	222
Hopkins, Samuel,	D. A. R. Lin. Book Vol. XXVI.,	32
Hoskin, Joseph,	Boyd's Annals,	61
*Hoyt, Nathaniel,	Rec. Conn. Men,	650
*Hubbell, Silliman,	Rec. Conn. Men,	653
Hudson, David,	Lists and Returns,	61
Hudson, George,	Boyd's Annals,	162, 163
	Rolls and Lists,	39
Hudson, George,	Lists and Returns,	84
*Hungerford, Reuben,	Boyd's Annals,	173
Hurlbut, Samuel,	Rec. Conn. Men,	81
	Boyd's Annals,	97
*Hurlbut, Stephen,	Rec. Conn. Men,	195, 539
	Lists and Returns,	60, 84, 243

LITCHFIELD COUNTY REVOLUTIONARY SOLDIERS

Name	Authority	Page
*Knowlton, Stephen,	Rec. Conn. Men,	
	Boyd's Annals,	46, 55
Leach, William, (Leatch)	Rec. Conn. Men,	162
	Boyd's Annals,	228, 647
	Rolls and Lists,	96, 163
	Lists and Returns,	39
*Loomis, Epaphras, Capt.,	See Torrington List.	60, 84
Loomis, Ichabod,	Lists and Returns,	
*Loomis, Wait,	D. A. R. Lin. Book Vol. XXV.,	362
	See Torrington List.	10
Lucas, William,	Rec. Conn. Men,	
	Boyd's Annals,	48
*Mallory, Amasa,	See Barkhamsted List.	162
*Marsh, John,	See Barkhamsted List.	
McCune, Robert, (McEwen)	Boyd's Annals,	
McCune, Sam'l, (McEwen)	Boyd's Annals,	57
Mills, David,	Rec. Conn. Men,	57
	Boyd's Annals,	562
Moore, Simeon, Jr.,	Boyd's Annals,	271
Moss, Samuel,	Rec. Conn. Men,	170
Mott, Adam, Jr.,	Rec. Conn. Men,	562
	Boyd's Annals,	63, 250
	Rolls and Lists,	38
Mott, Adam,	Lists and Returns,	39
Mott, Lent,	Boyd's Annals,	34, 60, 84
Mott, Samuel,	Rec. Conn. Men,	38
	Boyd's Annals,	298
*Norton, Levi,	See Goshen List.	162
Palmer, Benjamin,	Boyd's Annals,	
*Perkins, Abner,	Rolls and Lists,	160
Phelps, Elkanah,	Boyd's Annals,	202
*Platt, Ebenezer,	Rolls and Lists,	349, 352
Potter, David H.,	Lists and Returns,	104, 131
Potter, Phineas,	Boyd's Annals,	285
	Rolls and Lists,	269
Potter, Sheldon,	Rolls and Lists,	39
Preston, Jonathan,	Boyd's Annals,	121
	Lists and Returns,	147, 162
Preston, Joseph,	Boyd's Annals,	61, 84
	Rolls and Lists,	36, 147
Preston, Josiah,	Lists and Returns,	39
Preston, Samuel,	Lists and Returns,	281
Priest, Philip,	Boyd's Annals,	362
Prince, ———,	Boyd's Annals,	126, 217
Prince, Neagro,	Lists and Returns,	146
Roberts, Joel,	Rec. Conn. Men,	61, 84
	Boyd's Annals,	541
Roberts, Judah,	Rec. Conn. Men,	113
		541, 653

Name	Authority	Page
Roberts, Samuel,	Rec. Conn. Men,	570
	Boyd's Annals,	152, 162
	Lists and Returns,	188
Rogers, Simeon,	Rec. Conn. Men,	541
	Boyd's Annals,	284
Rowley, Ebenezer,	Boyd's Annals,	162, 276
*Russell, Nathaniel, Corp.,	Rec. Conn. Men,	25
	D. A. R. Lin. Book Vol. XXVII.,	323
Scoville, Ebenezer,	Lists and Returns,	211
Scovil, Stephen,	Boyd's Annals,	146
	Lists and Returns,	41, 61, 84, 175, 253
Smith, Josiah,	Boyd's Annals,	147, 267
Spencer, Thomas,	Boyd's Annals,	94
Stannard, Lemuel, Jr.,	Boyd's Annals,	162
Stannard, William,	Rec. Conn. Men,	163, 203, 562
	Boyd's Annals,	74, 161, 163
Stannard, Peabody,	Boyd's Annals,	162
	Lists and Returns,	61, 84
Stannard, Seth,	Rolls and Lists,	39, 122
	Rec. Conn. Men,	251, 336
	Lists and Returns,	61, 84
*Shattuck, Randall,	Boyd's Annals,	382
*Shattuck, William,	Rec. Conn. Men,	653
*Smith, Zebina, Capt.,	Rec. Conn. Men,	63, 653
	Boyd's Annals,	296
	Rolls and Lists,	67
*Sweet, John,	Boyd's Annals,	162, 288
Sweet, Jonathan,	Boyd's Annals,	108, 123
	Rolls and Lists,	37
Sweet, Peleg,	Rec. Conn. Men,	63, 203
	Boyd's Annals,	161
Tucker, Reuben,	Rec. Conn. Men,	502
*Wade, Stephen,	Rec. Conn. Men,	216, 340
Walter, Daniel,	Boyd's Annals,	162
*Walter, John,	Boyd's Annals,	275
Walter, Lemuel,	Rec. Conn. Men,	167
	Lists and Returns,	188
*West, Judah,	Rec. Conn. Men,	50
	Boyd's Annals,	162, 289
*Wheadon, Solomon,	Boyd's Annals,	194
†Wilcoxson, Gideon,	Rec. Conn. Men,	423
	Boyd's Annals,	108, 162
Wilkinson, Abraham,	Boyd's Annals,	161
Wilkinson, Levi,	Boyd's Annals,	162
	Lists and Returns,	61, 84
Wilkinson, Jesse,	Boyd's Annals,	162
	Lists and Returns,	44, 60, 84, 177
Woodruff, Hawkins,	Rec. Conn. Men,	63
	Boyd's Annals,	107, 161
Wright, Charles,	Rec. Conn. Men,	63
	Rolls and Lists,	21, 209

Name	Authority	Page
Wright, Daniel,	Lists and Returns,	213
Wright, David,	Rec. Conn. Men,	63
	Boyd's Annals,	264
Wright, Freedom,	Rec. Conn. Men,	63
	Boyd's Annals,	265
Wright, John, Lieut.,	Boyd's Annals,	263, 265
Wright, Moses,	Rec. Conn. Men,	167
	Rolls and Lists,	105

Woodbury

Revolutionary Soldiers

OF

Woodbury

COMPILED BY
JUDEA CHAPTER
DAUGHTERS OF THE AMERICAN REVOLUTION
WASHINGTON, CONN.

For fuller accounts of these men see original lists

Revolutionary Soldiers of Woodbury

Name	Authority	Page
Abernethy, James,	Cothren's Hist.,	779
Adge, Aner,	Cothren's Hist.,	779
Allen, Parmeley, Capt.,	Cothren's Hist.,	779
Allien, Samuel,	Cothren's Hist.,	779
Ambler, David,	Cothren's Hist.,	779
Andruss, Benj., Lieut.,	Cothren's Hist.,	779
Andruss, Thomas,	Cothren's Hist.,	779
Armstrong, Stephen,	Cothren's Hist.,	779
Armstrong, James,	Cothren's Hist.,	779
Arthur, James,	Cothren's Hist.,	779
Atwood, Asa,	Cothren's Hist.,	779
Atwood, Benj.,	Cothren's Hist.,	779
Austin, Caleb,	Cothren's Hist.,	779
Averel, Reuben,	Cothren's Hist.,	779
Avery, Benj.,	Cothren's Hist.,	779
Avery, Nathaniel,	Cothren's Hist.,	779
Ayer, Peter,	Cothren's Hist.,	779
Backus, Delucena,	Cothren's Hist.,	780
Bacon, Gould,	Cothren's Hist.,	779
Bacon, John,	Cothren's Hist.,	779
Bacon, Josiah,	Cothren's Hist.,	779
Bailey, Jonathan,	Cothren's Hist.,	779
Baker, Edward,	Cothren's Hist.,	779
Baker, Eldad,	Cothren's Hist.,	779
Baker, John,	Cothren's Hist.,	779
Baker, John, Jr.,	Cothren's Hist.,	779
Baker, Lovewell,	Cothren's Hist.,	779
Baker, Nathan,	Cothren's Hist.,	779
Baker, Phineas,	Cothren's Hist.,	779
Baker, Remember, Capt.,	Cothren's Hist.,	779
Baker, Thaddeus,	Cothren's Hist.,	779
Baldwin, Asahel,	Cothren's Hist.,	779
Baldwin, Enos, Jr.,	Cothren's Hist.,	779
Baldwin, Judah,	Cothren's Hist.,	779
Baldwin, Nathan,	Cothren's Hist.,	780
Banham, John,	Cothren's Hist.,	779
Bannister, George,	Cothren's Hist.,	780
Barlow, David,	Cothren's Hist.,	779
Barlow, John,	Cothren's Hist.,	779
Barnes, Abraham,	Cothren's Hist.,	780

Name	Authority	Page
Barnes, Frederick,	Cothren's Hist.,	780
Barnes, John,	Cothren's Hist.,	780
Barnes, Samuel,	Cothren's Hist.,	780
Barnes, Simeon,	Cothren's Hist.,	780
Bassett, Samuel,	Cothren's Hist.,	779
Bates, Elias,	Cothren's Hist.,	780
Beach, Ambrose,	Cothren's Hist.,	779
Beach, Curtiss,	Cothren's Hist.,	779
Beardsley, Henry,	Cothren's Hist.,	779
Beardsley, John,	Cothren's Hist.,	779
Beardsley, Nathan,	Cothren's Hist.,	779
Beardsley, Theodorus,	Cothren's Hist.,	779
Bedeau, William,	Cothren's Hist.,	779
Beecher, Abraham,	Cothren's Hist.,	779
Beemont, Friend,	Cothren's Hist.,	779
Beemont, William,	Cothren's Hist.,	779
Beers, Abner,	Cothren's Hist.,	780
Beers, Josiah,	Cothren's Hist.,	780
Beers, Lewis,	Cothren's Hist.,	780
Beers, Nathan, Lieut.,	Cothren's Hist.,	780
Beers, Philo,	Cothren's Hist.,	780
Beers, Silas,	Cothren's Hist.,	780
Beers, Stephen,	Cothren's Hist.,	780
Beers, Zachariah,	Cothren's Hist.,	780
Beldon, Asahel,	Cothren's Hist.,	779
Bellamy, Jonathan,	Cothren's Hist.,	779
Bell, Andrew,	Cothren's Hist.,	779
Bell, Benjamin,	Cothren's Hist.,	779
Benedict, William,	Cothren's Hist.,	780
Bird, Ebenezer,	Cothren's Hist.,	779
Blaisdell, Roger,	Cothren's Hist.,	780
Blakesley, Ezra,	Cothren's Hist.,	779
Blakesley, Filley, Capt.,	Cothren's Hist.,	779
Blakesley, Isaac,	Cothren's Hist.,	779
Blakesley, James,	Cothren's Hist.,	779
Blakesley, Jonathan,	Cothren's Hist.,	779
Blakesley, Joseph,	Cothren's Hist.,	779
Blenney, Barnabas,	Cothren's Hist.,	780
Bloom, Isaac,	Cothren's Hist.,	780
Blois, Edward,	Cothren's Hist.,	779
Bond, William,	Cothren's Hist.,	779
Booth, Aaron,	Cothren's Hist.,	779
Booth, Abijah,	Cothren's Hist.,	779
Booth, Amos,	Cothren's Hist.,	779
Booth, James, Capt.,	Cothren's Hist.,	779
Booth, John,	Cothren's Hist.,	779
Booth, Joseph,	Cothren's Hist.,	779

WOODBURY

Name	Authority	Page
Bostwick, Andrew,	Cothren's Hist.,	780
Botsford, Samuel,	Cothren's Hist.,	780
Brace, Joseph,	Cothren's Hist.,	779
Bradley, Jehiel,	Cothren's Hist.,	780
Bradley, Zuar,	Cothren's Hist.,	780
Brewster, Gideon,	Cothren's Hist.,	779
Brewster, Jonas,	Cothren's Hist.,	779
Brinsmade, Dan. N., Hon.,	Cothren's Hist.,	779
Brinsmade, Zechariah,	Cothren's Hist.,	779
Bristol, Gideon,	Cothren's Hist.,	779
Bristol, Nathaniel, Jr.,	Cothren's Hist.,	779
Brown, Asahel,	Cothren's Hist.,	779
Brown, Elijah,	Cothren's Hist.,	779
Brothwell, Joseph F.,	Cothren's Hist.,	779
Brownson, Abel,	Cothren's Hist.,	779
Brownson, Abijah, Sergt.,	Cothren's Hist.,	779
Brownson, Abraham,	Cothren's Hist.,	779
Brownson, Cornelius Bondy, Ensign,	Cothren's Hist.,	779
Brownson, Gideon, Capt.,	Cothren's Hist.,	779
Brownson, Luman,	Cothren's Hist.,	779
Brownson, Thomas,	Cothren's Hist.,	779
Buel, Benjamin,	Cothren's Hist.,	779
Bulford, John,	Cothren's Hist.,	779
Bull, Thomas, Maj.,	Cothren's Hist.,	779
Bullard, Isaac,	Cothren's Hist.,	779
Bunce, Isaiah,	Cothren's Hist.,	779
Bunce, John,	Cothren's Hist.,	779
Bunnell, Frederick,	Cothren's Hist.,	779
Burchard, Dan,	Cothren's Hist.,	780
Burns, John,	Cothren's Hist.,	779
Burr, William, Sergt.,	Cothren's Hist.,	780
Burritt, Anthony, Dr.,	Cothren's Hist.,	780
Burritt, Samuel,	Cothren's Hist.,	780
Burton, Asahel,	Cothren's Hist.,	779
Burton, Daniel,	Cothren's Hist.,	779
Burton, David,	Cothren's Hist.,	779
Burton, Ephraim,	Cothren's Hist.,	779
Burton, Jeremiah,	Cothren's Hist.,	779
Burton, Judson, Ensign,	Cothren's Hist.,	779
Burton, Robert,	Cothren's Hist.,	779
Burton, William,	Cothren's Hist.,	779
Calechan, Thomas,	Cothren's Hist.,	780
Camp, David, Ensign,	Cothren's Hist.,	780
*Camp, Phineas,	Lists and Returns,	26
Canfield, Elisha,	Cothren's Hist.,	780
Canfield, Thomas,	Cothren's Hist.,	780

Carpenter, William, H.,	Cothren's Hist.,	780
Carter, John,	Cothren's Hist.,	780
Case, John C.,	Cothren's Hist.,	780
Castle, John,	Cothren's Hist.,	780
Castle, Timothy,	Cothren's Hist.,	780
Chapman, Israel,	Cothren's Hist.,	780
Chapman, Nathan, Capt.,	Cothren's Hist.,	780
Chatfield, Yarmouth,	Cothren's Hist.,	780
Chidson, John,	Cothren's Hist.,	780
Chilman, Thomas,	Cothren's Hist.,	780
Chilson, Thomas,	Cothren's Hist.,	780
Chittenden, Daniel,	Cothren's Hist.,	780
*Church, Ebenezer,	Cothren's Hist.,	780
Church, Moses,	Cothren's Hist.,	780
Church, Nathaniel,	Cothren's Hist.,	780
Churchill, Moses,	Cothren's Hist.,	780
Clark, Amos,	Cothren's Hist.,	780
Clark, Benjamin,	Cothren's Hist.,	780
Clark, Isaac,	Cothren's Hist.,	780
Clark, John,	Cothren's Hist.,	780
Clark, Josiah,	Cothren's Hist.,	780
Clark, Phineas,	Cothren's Hist.,	780
Clark, Robert,	Cothren's Hist.,	780
Clark, William,	Cothren's Hist.,	780
Coflin, Samuel,	Cothren's Hist.,	780
Cogswell, William, Capt.,	Cothren's Hist.,	780
Cole, Phineas,	Cothren's Hist.,	780
Cole, Simeon,	Cothren's Hist.,	780
Coles, Amos,	Cothren's Hist.,	780
Coles, James,	Cothren's Hist.,	780
Collins, Edward, Ensign,	Cothren's Hist.,	780
Corbran, Samuel,	Cothren's Hist.,	780
Couch, Ebenezer, Capt.,	Cothren's Hist.,	780
Cowles, Asa,	See original list.	
Crammer, John,	Cothren's Hist.,	780
Crissey, Truman,	Cothren's Hist.,	780
Crissey, Solomon,	Cothren's Hist.,	780
Crosby, ———,	Cothren's Hist.,	780
Crow, Elias,	Cothren's Hist.,	780
Crowfoot, James,	Cothren's Hist.,	780
Curtiss, Aaron,	Cothren's Hist.,	780
Curtiss, Abner,	Cothren's Hist.,	780
Curtiss, Agur, Capt.,	Cothren's Hist.,	780
Curtiss, Andrew,	Cothren's Hist.,	780
Curtiss, Asa,	Cothren's Hist.,	780
Curtiss, Daniel,	Cothren's Hist.,	780
Curtiss, David,	Cothren's Hist.,	780
Curtiss, Ebenezer,	Cothren's Hist.,	780

Name	Authority	Page
Curtiss, Edmund,	Cothren's Hist.,	780
Curtiss, Eleazur, Capt.,	Cothren's Hist.,	780
Curtiss, Elihu,	Cothren's Hist.,	780
Curtiss, Ephraim, Lieut.,	Cothren's Hist.,	780
Curtiss, Henry,	Cothren's Hist.,	780
Curtiss, Isaac,	Cothren's Hist.,	780
Curtiss, Israel, Jr.,	Cothren's Hist.,	780
Curtiss, Jabez,	Cothren's Hist.,	780
Curtiss, Jeremiah,	Cothren's Hist.,	780
Curtiss, Lewis,	Cothren's Hist.,	780
Curtiss, Phineas,	Cothren's Hist.,	780
Curtiss, Reuben,	Cothren's Hist.,	780
Curtiss, Robert,	Cothren's Hist.,	780
Curtiss, Wait,	Cothren's Hist.,	780
Cutler, Joseph,	Cothren's Hist.,	780
Dally, Obadiah,	Cothren's Hist.,	780
Davenport, Jonathan,	Cothren's Hist.,	780
Davidson, John,	Cothren's Hist.,	780
Davis, Amos,	Cothren's Hist.,	780
De Forest, Joseph,	Cothren's Hist.,	780
Dimonds, David,	Cothren's Hist.,	780
Dimonds, John,	Cothren's Hist.,	780
Dixon, Archibald,	Cothren's Hist.,	780
Dixon, David,	Cothren's Hist.,	780
Dixon, Jared,	Cothren's Hist.,	780
Doel, Shem,	Cothren's Hist.,	780
Doolittle, Thomas,	Cothren's Hist.,	780
Downs, Daniel,	Cothren's Hist.,	780
Downs, Eliphalet,	Cothren's Hist.,	780
Dunning, Christopher,	Cothren's Hist.,	780
Dunning, David,	Cothren's Hist.,	780
Dunning, Elias, Capt., Commissary,	Cothren's Hist.,	780
Dunning, Phineas,	Cothren's Hist.,	780
Dudley, Buel,	Cothren's Hist.,	780
Dudley, Benjamin,	Cothren's Hist.,	780
Dudley, Elizur,	Cothren's Hist.,	780
Dudley, George,	Cothren's Hist.,	780
Dudley, Nathan,	Cothren's Hist.,	780
Durbey, Ephraim,	Cothren's Hist.,	780
Durbey, John,	Cothren's Hist.,	780
Durkee, Asa,	Cothren's Hist.,	780
Durkee, Benjamin,	Cothren's Hist.,	780
Eastburn, Deliverance,	Cothren's Hist.,	781
Eastman, Azariah,	Cothren's Hist.,	781
Eastman, Benjamin,	Cothren's Hist.,	781
Easton, Elijah,	Cothren's Hist.,	781

LITCHFIELD COUNTY REVOLUTIONARY SOLDIERS

Name	Authority	Page
Easton, Eliphalet,	Lists and Returns,	28
Easton, Julian,	Cothren's Hist.,	781
Easton, Normand,	Cothren's Hist.,	781
Edmond, William,	Cothren's Hist.,	781
Edwards, John, Corp.,	Cothren's Hist.,	781
Elderkin, Jedediah,	Cothren's Hist.,	781
Elgur, Abner,	Cothren's Hist.,	781
Ellis, Jonas,	Cothren's Hist.,	781
Elwood, ———,	Cothren's Hist.,	781
Fales, Francis,	Cothren's Hist.,	781
Fall, Patrick,	Cothren's Hist.,	781
Farrand, Jonathan, Capt.,	Cothren's Hist.,	781
Fenn, Daniel,	Cothren's Hist.,	781
Field, Francis,	Cothren's Hist.,	781
Field, George,	Cothren's Hist.,	781
Fieldsley, Francis,	Cothren's Hist.,	781
*Filets, Francis,	Cothren's Hist.,	781
Fish, Nathan,	Cothren's Hist.,	781
Fisher, Darius,	Cothren's Hist.,	781
Flowers, Nathan,	Cothren's Hist.,	781
Flowers, Nathaniel,	Cothren's Hist.,	781
Foot, Joseph,	Cothren's Hist.,	781
Franklin, Jehiel,	Cothren's Hist.,	781
	Lists and Returns,	29
Frisbie, Abiel,	Cothren's Hist.,	781
Frisbie, Asahel,	Cothren's Hist.,	781
Frisbie, David,	Cothren's Hist.,	781
Frisbie, James,	Cothren's Hist.,	781
Frisbie, Jonathan,	Cothren's Hist.,	781
Frisbie, Noah,	Cothren's Hist.,	781
Frisbie, Noah, Jr.,	Cothren's Hist.,	781
Frost, Joseph,	Cothren's Hist.,	781
Gage, Thomas,	Cothren's Hist.,	781
Galesley, Thomas,	Cothren's Hist.,	781
Galpin, Joseph,	Cothren's Hist.,	781
Galpin, Samuel,	Cothren's Hist.,	781
Galpin, Stephen,	Cothren's Hist.,	781
Gardin, John,	Cothren's Hist.,	781
Garnet, John,	Cothren's Hist.,	781
Garnsey, Joseph,	Cothren's Hist.,	781
Garret, John,	Cothren's Hist.,	781
Garret, Jolin,	Cothren's Hist.,	781
Gear, Ezra,	Cothren's Hist.,	781
Gideons, Joshua,	Cothren's Hist.,	781
Gilbert, Elnathan,	Cothren's Hist.,	781
Gillet, David,	Cothren's Hist.,	781
Gillet, Eliphalet,	Cothren's Hist.,	781

WOODBURY

Name	Authority	Page
Gilchrist, ———,	Cothren's Hist.,	781
Gilbert, Isaiah, Corp.,	Cothren's Hist.,	781
Gillis, Fint, (Tint)	Cothren's Hist.,	781
	Lists and Returns,	61
Giteau, Simeon,	Rec. Conn. Men,	468
Glazier, Jacob,	Cothren's Hist.,	781
Goodrich, Timothy,	Cothren's Hist.,	781
Goodrich, Wait, Com'sary,	Cothren's Hist.,	781
Goodsell, Isaac,	Cothren's Hist.,	781
Gordon, Robert,	Cothren's Hist.,	781
Gorham, Benjamin,	Cothren's Hist.,	781
Gould, John W.,	Cothren's Hist.,	781
Graham, Andrew, Surg.,	Cothren's Hist.,	781
Graham, Chauncey, Chap.,	Cothren's Hist.,	781
Graham, Isaac G., Surg.,	Cothren's Hist.,	781
Grant, Elisha,	Cothren's Hist.,	781
Green, Eleazer,	Cothren's Hist.,	781
Green, Ezra,	Cothren's Hist.,	781
Green, Samuel,	Cothren's Hist.,	781
Gridley, Asahel,	Cothren's Hist.,	781
Griswold, Ebenezer,	Cothren's Hist.,	781
Guernsey, Richard,	Cothren's Hist.,	781
Guernsey, Solomon,	Cothren's Hist.,	781
Hall, Aaron,	Cothren's Hist.,	782
Hall, Ebenezer,	Cothren's Hist.,	782
Hall, L.,	Cothren's Hist.,	782
Hall, Thomas,	Cothren's Hist.,	782
Hall, Thomas, Jr.,	Cothren's Hist.,	782
Hand, Elias,	Cothren's Hist.,	782
Hannah, Alexander,	Cothren's Hist.,	782
Hannah, James,	Cothren's Hist.,	782
Hannah, Robert,	Cothren's Hist.,	782
Hannayed, William,	Cothren's Hist.,	782
Hamsted, David,	Cothren's Hist.,	782
Hastians, Samuel,	Cothren's Hist.,	782
Hastings, Seth, Surg.,	Cothren's Hist.,	782
Hawkins, Moses,	Cothren's Hist.,	782
Hawkins, Zadock,	Cothren's Hist.,	782
Hawkins, Zadock, Jr.,	Cothren's Hist.,	782
Hawley, David,	Cothren's Hist.,	782
Hawley, Enos, Capt.,	Cothren's Hist.,	782
Hawley, James,	Cothren's Hist.,	782
Hawley, Moses,	Cothren's Hist.,	782
Hayes, ———,	Cothren's Hist.,	782
Hazen, Elijah, Sergt.,	Cothren's Hist.,	782
Hazen, William,	Cothren's Hist.,	782
Henries, Zadock,	Cothren's Hist.,	782

Name	Authority	Page
Herrick, John,	Cothren's Hist.,	782
Hicock, Asa,	Cothren's Hist.,	782
Hicock, Benjamin,	Cothren's Hist.,	782
Hicock, David,	Cothren's Hist.,	782
Hicock, Ebenezer,	Cothren's Hist.,	782
Hicock, Elijah,	Cothren's Hist.,	782
Hicock, Ephraim,	Cothren's Hist.,	782
Hicock, Johnson,	Cothren's Hist.,	782
Hicock, Nathaniel,	Cothren's Hist.,	782
Hicock, Reuben,	Cothren's Hist.,	782
Hicock, Silas,	Cothren's Hist.,	782
Hicock, Thaddeus, Jr.,	Cothren's Hist.,	782
Higley, Nehemiah,	Cothren's Hist.,	782
Hilliard, William,	Cothren's Hist.,	782
Hill, Abraham,	Cothren's Hist.,	782
Hill, Reuben,	Cothren's Hist.,	782
Hill, Solomon,	Cothren's Hist.,	782
Hine, Adam,	Cothren's Hist.,	782
Hine, Jonathan,	Cothren's Hist.,	782
Hine, Lewis,	Cothren's Hist.,	782
Hine, Nathan, Capt.,	Cothren's Hist.,	782
Hinman, Asa, Lieut.,	Cothren's Hist.,	781
Hinman, Benjamin, Col.,	Cothren's Hist.,	781
Hinman, Benjamin, 3rd,	Cothren's Hist.,	781
Hinman, Daniel,	Cothren's Hist.,	781
Hinman, David, Capt.,	Cothren's Hist.,	781
Hinman, Elijah, Capt.,	Cothren's Hist.,	781
Hinman, Elisha, Capt.,	Cothren's Hist.,	782
Hinman, Enos,	Cothren's Hist.,	781
Hinman, Enos,	Cothren's Hist.,	781
Hinman, Ephraim, Capt., Com.,	Cothren's Hist.,	781
Hinman, Francis,	Cothren's Hist.,	781
Hinman, Isaiah,	Cothren's Hist.,	781
Hinman, James,	Cothren's Hist.,	781
Hinman, Joel, Ensign,	Cothren's Hist.,	781
Hinman, Jonas,	Cothren's Hist.,	781
Hinman, Lemuel,	Cothren's Hist.,	781
Hinman, Michael,	Cothren's Hist.,	781
Hinman, Moses,	Cothren's Hist.,	781
Hinman, Samuel, Capt.,	Cothren's Hist.,	781
Hinman, Silas,	Cothren's Hist.,	781
Hinman, Timothy,	Cothren's Hist.,	781
Hinman, Titus, Ensign,	Cothren's Hist.,	782
Hinman, Truman, Capt., Commissary,	Cothren's Hist.,	781
Hinman, Wait,	Cothren's Hist.,	781

Name	Authority	Page
Hitchcock, Benjamin,	Cothren's Hist.,	782
Hitchcock, Benjamin, Jr.,	Cothren's Hist.,	782
Hitchcock, David,	Cothren's Hist.,	782
Hitchcock, James R.,	Cothren's Hist.,	782
Hobert, Elisha,	Cothren's Hist.,	782
Hobert, John,	Cothren's Hist.,	782
Hodge, Gulielmus,	Cothren's Hist.,	782
Hodge, Philo,	Cothren's Hist.,	782
Hooker, James,	Cothren's Hist.,	782
Hooker, Thaddeus,	Cothren's Hist.,	782
Hotchkiss, Reuben,	Cothren's Hist.,	782
Hows, George,	Cothren's Hist.,	782
Hows, Samuel,	Cothren's Hist.,	782
Hubbell, Ebenezer,	Cothren's Hist.,	782
Hull, Ebenezer,	Cothren's Hist.,	782
Hull, Stephen,	Cothren's Hist.,	782
Hull, Titus, Surg.,	Cothren's Hist.,	782
Hull, William,	Cothren's Hist.,	782
Humphrey, Elijah, Capt.,	Cothren's Hist.,	782
Hungerford, Benjamin, Lt.,	Cothren's Hist.,	782
Hunt, Isaac,	Cothren's Hist.,	782
Hunt, Isaac, Jr.,	Cothren's Hist.,	782
Hunt, John,	Cothren's Hist.,	782
Hunt, Simeon,	Cothren's Hist.,	782
Huntington, Ebenezer,	Cothren's Hist.,	782
Hurd, Abner,	Cothren's Hist.,	782
Hurd, Abraham,	Cothren's Hist.,	782
Hurd, Adam, Capt.,	Cothren's Hist.,	782
Hurd, Asahel, Lieut.,	Cothren's Hist.,	782
Hurd, Calvin,	Cothren's Hist.,	782
Hurd, Curtiss,	Cothren's Hist.,	782
Hurd, Daniel,	Cothren's Hist.,	782
Hurd, David, Capt.,	Cothren's Hist.,	782
Hurd, David, Jr.,	Cothren's Hist.,	782
Hurd, Gideon,	Cothren's Hist.,	782
Hurd, Gideon, Jr.,	Cothren's Hist.,	782
Hurd, Graham,	Cothren's Hist.,	782
Hurd, Isaac,	Cothren's Hist.,	782
Hurd, John,	Cothren's Hist.,	782
Hurd, Joseph,	Cothren's Hist.,	782
Hurd, Lewis,	Cothren's Hist.,	782
Hurd, Lovewell,	Cothren's Hist.,	782
Hurd, Moses,	Cothren's Hist.,	782
Hurd, Noah,	Cothren's Hist.,	782
Hurd, Samuel,	Cothren's Hist.,	782
Hurd, Simeon,	Cothren's Hist.,	782
Hurd, Simeon, Jr.,	Cothren's Hist.,	782

Litchfield County Revolutionary Soldiers

Name	Authority	Page
Hurd, Stephen,	Cothren's Hist.,	782
Hurd, Solomon,	Cothren's Hist.,	782
Hurd, Thaddeus, Capt.,	Cothren's Hist.,	782
Hurlbut, Abraham,	Cothren's Hist.,	782
Hurlbut, Adam, Capt.,	Cothren's Hist.,	782
Hurlbut, Amos,	Cothren's Hist.,	782
Hurlbut, Asaph,	Cothren's Hist.,	782
Hurlbut, Elisha,	Cothren's Hist.,	782
Hurlbut, Gideon,	Cothren's Hist.,	782
Hurlbut, Gideon, Jr.,	Cothren's Hist.,	782
Hurlbut, Joel,	Cothren's Hist.,	782
Hurlbut, Joel,	Cothren's Hist.,	782
Hurlbut, John,	Cothren's Hist.,	782
Hurlbut, Noah,	Cothren's Hist.,	782
Hurlbut, Robert,	Cothren's Hist.,	782
Hurlbut, Samuel, Capt.,	Cothren's Hist.,	782
Hurlbut, Squire,	Cothren's Hist.,	782
Hurlbut, Thomas,	Cothren's Hist.,	782
Hurlbut, Truman,	Cothren's Hist.,	782
Hurlbut, Wait,	Cothren's Hist.,	782
Indian, Tom,	Cothren's Hist.,	782
Ingraham, Eleazer,	Cothren's Hist.,	782
Ingraham, Henry,	Cothren's Hist.,	782
Ingraham, Nathaniel,	Cothren's Hist.,	782
Ingraham, William,	Cothren's Hist.,	782
Isbell, Seruda,	Cothren's Hist.,	782
Ives, Abner,	Cothren's Hist.,	782
Ives, Asahel,	Cothren's Hist.,	782
Ives, Daniel, Jr.,	Cothren's Hist.,	782
Jackson, Samuel,	Cothren's Hist.,	783
Jackson, Theophilus,	Cothren's Hist.,	783
James, Thomas,	Cothren's Hist.,	783
Jennings, Charles,	Cothren's Hist.,	783
Jenks, Thomas,	Cothren's Hist.,	783
Jewett, Isaac,	Cothren's Hist.,	783
Jones, Benjamin,	Cothren's Hist.,	783
Johnson, Hiram,	Cothren's Hist.,	783
Johnson, Isaac,	Cothren's Hist.,	783
Johnson, Isaiah,	Cothren's Hist.,	783
Johnson, John,	Cothren's Hist.,	783
Johnson, Justus,	Cothren's Hist.,	783
Johnson, Peter,	Cothren's Hist.,	783
Johnson, William,	Cothren's Hist.,	783
Jordan, John,	Cothren's Hist.,	783
Jordan, William,	Cothren's Hist.,	783
Judd, Daniel,	Cothren's Hist.,	783
Judd, Freeman,	Cothren's Hist.,	783

Name	Authority	Page
Judson, Aaron,	Cothren's Hist.,	783
Judson, Abel,	Cothren's Hist.,	783
Judson, Agur,	Cothren's Hist.,	783
Judson, Amos, Ensign,	Cothren's Hist.,	783
Judson, Chapman, Sr.,	Cothren's Hist.,	783
Judson, Chapman, Jr.,	Cothren's Hist.,	783
Judson, Elihu,	Cothren's Hist.,	783
Judson, Elijah,	Cothren's Hist.,	783
Judson, James, Capt.,	Cothren's Hist.,	783
Judson, James,	Cothren's Hist.,	783
Judson, Joel,	Cothren's Hist.,	783
Judson, John, Ensign,	Cothren's Hist.,	783
Judson, Joseph,	Cothren's Hist.,	783
Judson, Joshua,	Cothren's Hist.,	783
Judson, Timothy, Capt.,	Cothren's Hist.,	783
Judson, William,	Cothren's Hist.,	783
Kasson, Alexander,	Cothren's Hist.,	783
Kasson, Archibald,	Cothren's Hist.,	783
Kasson, James,	Cothren's Hist.,	783
Keeler, Hezekiah,	Cothren's Hist.,	783
Keeney, Levi,	Cothren's Hist.,	783
Kellis, Peter,	Cothren's Hist.,	783
Kelly, John,	Cothren's Hist.,	783
Kimberly, David,	Cothren's Hist.,	783
Kimberly, Thomas,	Cothren's Hist.,	783
Knapp, Eleazer,	Cothren's Hist.,	783
Knapp, Moses,	Cothren's Hist.,	783
Lacey, Ebenezer,	Cothren's Hist.,	783
Lacey, Ebenezer, Jr.,	Cothren's Hist.,	783
Lacey, Ezra,	Cothren's Hist.,	783
Lacey, Thaddeus, Capt.,	Cothren's Hist.,	783
Ladd, Benajah,	Cothren's Hist.,	783
Ladd, David,	Cothren's Hist.,	783
Lake, Edward,	Cothren's Hist.,	783
Lamfear, Samuel,	Cothren's Hist.,	783
Laslin, John,	Cothren's Hist.,	783
Lee, Abner,	Cothren's Hist.,	783
Lee, Samuel,	Cothren's Hist.,	783
Leavenworth, Amos,	Cothren's Hist.,	783
Leavenworth, David, Capt.,	Cothren's Hist.,	783
Leavenworth, David, Jr.,	Cothren's Hist.,	783
Leavenworth, Ebenezer, Lt.,	Cothren's Hist.,	783
Leavenworth, Gideon,	Cothren's Hist.,	783
Leavenworth, John, Capt.,	Cothren's Hist.,	783
Leavenworth, Morse,	Cothren's Hist.,	783
Leavitt, Daniel,	Cothren's Hist.,	783
Leavitt, Jonathan,	Cothren's Hist.,	783

Name	Authority	Page
Leavitt, Samuel,	Cothren's Hist.,	783
Lewis, Abraham,	Cothren's Hist.,	783
Lewis, Asa,	Cothren's Hist.,	783
Lewis, Elihu,	Cothren's Hist.,	783
Lewis, Ezekiel, Capt.,	Cothren's Hist.,	783
Lewis, George,	Cothren's Hist.,	783
Lewis, James,	Cothren's Hist.,	783
Lewis, Nathaniel,	Cothren's Hist.,	783
Liberty, Jeff,	Cothren's Hist.,	783
Lines, Abraham,	Cothren's Hist.,	783
Linsley, Abiel,	Cothren's Hist.,	783
Linsley, Abiel, Jr.,	Cothren's Hist.,	783
Linsley, Brainerd,	Cothren's Hist.,	783
Logan, John,	Cothren's Hist.,	783
Logan, Matthew,	Cothren's Hist.,	783
London, Pomp,	Cothren's Hist.,	783
Lusk, Samuel,	Cothren's Hist.,	783
Lyon, Isaac,	Cothren's Hist.,	783
MacDaniel, Thomas,	Cothren's Hist.,	784
Mallory, Aaron, Aide to Washington,	Cothren's Hist.,	784
Mallory, Abner, Capt.,	Cothren's Hist.,	784
Mallory, Daniel,	Cothren's Hist.,	784
Mallory, David,	Cothren's Hist.,	784
Mallory, Eli,	Cothren's Hist.,	784
Mallory, Hugh,	Cothren's Hist.,	784
Mallory, John,	Cothren's Hist.,	784
Mallory, John, Jr.,	Cothren's Hist.,	784
Mallory, Noah,	Cothren's Hist.,	784
Mallory, Samuel,	Cothren's Hist.,	784
Mallory, Simeon,	Cothren's Hist.,	784
Mallory, Walker,	Cothren's Hist.,	784
Manville, Ira,	Cothren's Hist.,	784
Manville, John,	Cothren's Hist.,	784
Manville, Simeon,	Cothren's Hist.,	784
Mansfield, Clement,	Cothren's Hist.,	784
Martin, Amos,	Cothren's Hist.,	783
Martin, Andrew, Capt.,	Cothren's Hist.,	783
Martin, David,	Cothren's Hist.,	783
Martin, Ezekiel,	Cothren's Hist.,	783
Martin, Gideon,	Cothren's Hist.,	783
Martin, Isaiah,	Cothren's Hist.,	783
Martin, Joel,	Cothren's Hist.,	783
Martin, Joseph,	Cothren's Hist.,	783
Martin, Samuel,	Cothren's Hist.,	783
Martin, Solomon,	Cothren's Hist.,	783
Martin, William,	Cothren's Hist.,	783

Name	Authority	Page
Masters, N. S.,	Cothren's Hist.,	784
McGrau, John,	Cothren's Hist.,	784
McKinney, John,	Cothren's Hist.,	784
Meigs, Jesse,	Cothren's Hist.,	784
Meigs, John, Sr.,	See original list.	
Merchant, Job,	Cothren's Hist.,	784
Meramble, John,	Cothren's Hist.,	784
Mills, Alexander,	Cothren's Hist.,	784
Mills, Curtiss,	Cothren's Hist.,	784
Mills, Samuel,	Cothren's Hist.,	784
Miner, Adoniram,	Cothren's Hist.,	783
Minor, Daniel,	Cothren's Hist.,	783
Minor, David,	Cothren's Hist.,	783
Minor, Elisha,	Cothren's Hist.,	783
Minor, Israel, Sergt.,	Cothren's Hist.,	783
Minor, Simeon,	Cothren's Hist.,	783
Minor, Timothy,	Cothren's Hist.,	783
Mitchel, Benjah,	Cothren's Hist.,	784
Mitchel, Daniel,	Cothren's Hist.,	784
Mitchel, David,	Cothren's Hist.,	784
Mitchel, Nathan,	Cothren's Hist.,	784
Mitchell, Abijah,	Cothren's Hist.,	784
Mitchell, Brier,	Cothren's Hist.,	784
Mitchell, Elezear, Capt.,	Cothren's Hist.,	784
Mitchell, Jehiel,	Cothren's Hist.,	784
Mitchell, John, Capt.,	Cothren's Hist.,	784
Mitchell, Nathaniel, Capt.,	Cothren's Hist.,	784
Mitchell, Seth,	Cothren's Hist.,	784
Mitchell, Simeon,	Cothren's Hist.,	784
Mitchell, Thomas,	Cothren's Hist.,	784
Mix, Joseph,	Cothren's Hist.,	784
Moody, Zimri,	Cothren's Hist.,	784
Moltrope, Jude,	Cothren's Hist.,	784
Morris, Matthew,	Cothren's Hist.,	784
Morgan, Lewis,	Cothren's Hist.,	784
Moseley, Abner, Capt.,	Cothren's Hist.,	783
Moseley, Increase, Esq., Commissary,	Cothren's Hist.,	783
Moseley, Increase, Jr., Col.,	Cothren's Hist.,	783
Mott, Lyman,	Cothren's Hist.,	784
Mulatto, Job,	Cothren's Hist.,	784
Mulatto, Michael,	Cothren's Hist.,	784
Munger, Jonathan,	Cothren's Hist.,	784
Munn, Ebenezer, Surg.,	Cothren's Hist.,	784
Munn, Justus,	Cothren's Hist.,	784
Munn, Samuel, Corp.,	Cothren's Hist.,	784
Murray, Hugh,	Cothren's Hist.,	784

LITCHFIELD COUNTY REVOLUTIONARY SOLDIERS

Name	Authority	Page
Murray, Noah,	Cothren's Hist.,	784
Murray, Samuel,	Cothren's Hist.,	784
My, Ebenezer,	Cothren's Hist.,	784
Nails, John,	Cothren's Hist.,	784
Negro, Cumming,	Cothren's Hist.,	784
Negro, James,	Cothren's Hist.,	784
Negro, Peter,	Cothren's Hist.,	784
Negro, Robbin,	Cothren's Hist.,	784
Negro, Titus,	Cothren's Hist.,	784
Negro, Toney,	Cothren's Hist.,	784
Nettleton, Josiah,	Cothren's Hist.,	784
Newton, Ezekiel,	Cothren's Hist.,	784
Nichols, Andrew,	Cothren's Hist.,	784
Nichols, Elisha,	Cothren's Hist.,	784
Nichols, James,	Cothren's Hist.,	784
Norton, David,	Cothren's Hist.,	784
Norton, George,	Cothren's Hist.,	784
Norton, George, Jr.,	Cothren's Hist.,	784
Norton, Issachar,	Cothren's Hist.,	784
Norton, John Austin,	Cothren's Hist.,	784
Norton, William,	Cothren's Hist.,	784
Olcott, John E.,	Cothren's Hist.,	784
Olds, Aaron,	Cothren's Hist.,	784
Olds, Oliver,	Cothren's Hist.,	784
Osborne, Nathan,	Cothren's Hist.,	784
Osborne, Samuel,	Cothren's Hist.,	784
Osborne, Shadrach, Com.,	Cothren's Hist.,	784
Pain, Justus,	Cothren's Hist.,	784
Palmer, Phineas,	Cothren's Hist.,	784
Parker, Amasa,	Cothren's Hist.,	784
Parker, Gamaliel,	Cothren's Hist.,	784
Parker, Peter,	Cothren's Hist.,	784
Parker, Thomas,	Cothren's Hist.,	784
Parks, James,	Cothren's Hist.,	784
Parmely, Thomas,	Cothren's Hist.,	784
Parry, Daniel,	Cothren's Hist.,	784
Patterson, William, Ensign,	Cothren's Hist.,	784
Patterson, Sherman,	Cothren's Hist.,	784
Pease, William,	Cothren's Hist.,	784
Peck, Abijah,	Cothren's Hist.,	784
Peet, Daniel,	Cothren's Hist.,	784
Peet, Richard,	Cothren's Hist.,	784
Perry, Charles,	Cothren's Hist.,	784
Perry, Eli,	Cothren's Hist.,	784
Perry, Elisha,	Cothren's Hist.,	784
Perry, Samuel,	Cothren's Hist.,	784
Pierce, David,	Cothren's Hist.,	784

WOODBURY

Name	Authority	Page
Pislie, Elijah,	Cothren's Hist.,	784
Pitcher, Ebenezer,	Cothren's Hist.,	784
Platt, John,	Cothren's Hist.,	784
Pollard, Isaac,	Cothren's Hist.,	784
Porter, Benjamin,	Cothren's Hist.,	784
Porter, David,	Cothren's Hist.,	784
Porter, Robert,	See original list.	
Post, Abraham,	Cothren's Hist.,	784
Potter, David,	Cothren's Hist.,	784
Prentice, Zachariah,	Cothren's Hist.,	784
Preston, Nathan, Paym'st'r.,	Cothren's Hist.,	784
Preston, Stephen,	See original list.	
Prindle, Enos,	Cothren's Hist.,	784
Pritchard, Nath.,	Cothren's Hist.,	784
Ranney, Solomon,	Cothren's Hist.,	785
Ranney, Stephen,	Cothren's Hist.,	785
Read, Jonathan,	Cothren's Hist.,	785
Read, Matthew,	Cothren's Hist.,	785
Reynolds, David,	Cothren's Hist.,	785
Reynolds, Hezekiah,	Cothren's Hist.,	785
Reynolds, James, Sergt.,	Cothren's Hist.,	785
Reynolds, James Blakesley,	Cothren's Hist.,	785
Reynolds, Justus,	Cothren's Hist.,	785
Reynolds, Matthew,	Cothren's Hist.,	785
Reynolds, Simeon,	Cothren's Hist.,	785
Reynolds, Solomon,	Cothren's Hist.,	785
Reynolds, Solomon, Jr.,	Cothren's Hist.,	785
Reynolds, William,	Cothren's Hist.,	785
Rice, Edward,	Cothren's Hist.,	785
Richards, Amos,	Cothren's Hist.,	785
Rill, Edward,	Cothren's Hist.,	785
Robin, Michael,	Cothren's Hist.,	785
Robinson, David,	Cothren's Hist.,	785
Robinson, Solomon,	Cothren's Hist.,	785
Robinson William,	Cothren's Hist.,	785
Rogers, Ebenezer,	Cothren's Hist.,	785
Rood, Simeon,	Cothren's Hist.,	785
Roots, Colonel,	Cothren's Hist.,	785
Roots, Joseph,	Cothren's Hist.,	785
Royce, Matthew,	Cothren's Hist.,	785
Rumrill, Frederick,	Cothren's Hist.,	785
Rumsey, David,	Cothren's Hist.,	785
Rumsey, Nathan,	Cothren's Hist.,	785
Rusco, Benjamin,	Cothren's Hist.,	785
Rusco, Stephen,	Cothren's Hist.,	785
Sanford, J., Capt.,	Cothren's Hist.,	785
Savage, Joseph,	Cothren's Hist.,	785

LITCHFIELD COUNTY REVOLUTIONARY SOLDIERS

Name	Authority	Page
Savage, Seth,	Cothren's Hist.,	785
Saxton, Jo,	Cothren's Hist.,	785
Sears, John,	Cothren's Hist.,	786
Seeley, Ephraim,	Cothren's Hist.,	786
Sedgwick, Archer,	Cothren's Hist.,	786
Sedgwick, Benjamin,	Cothren's Hist.,	786
Sedgwick, Joseph,	Cothren's Hist.,	786
Sharp, James,	Cothren's Hist.,	785
Sheldon, Charles,	Cothren's Hist.,	785
Sheldon, Daniel, Surgeon's mate,	Cothren's Hist.,	785
Sherman, David, Com.,	Cothren's Hist.,	786
Sherman, Daniel, Mem. Council Safety,	Cothren's Hist.,	786
Sherman, Elijah,	Cothren's Hist.,	786
Sherman, James,	Cothren's Hist.,	786
Sherman, John, Lieut.,	Cothren's Hist.,	786
Sherman, Taylor, Expressman,	Cothren's Hist.,	786
Simons, Cummey,	Cothren's Hist.,	786
Skeels, Adoniram,	Cothren's Hist.,	786
Skilton, Henry, Dr.,	Cothren's Hist.,	786
Slauter, John,	Cothren's Hist.,	785
†Smith, Daniel,	Cothren's Hist.,	785
Smith, Ebenezer, Capt.,	Cothren's Hist.,	785
Smith, Elisha,	Cothren's Hist.,	785
Smith, Jeremiah,	Cothren's Hist.,	785
Smith, Nathaniel, Hon.,	Cothren's Hist.,	785
Smith, Phineas,	Cothren's Hist.,	785
Smith, Richard, Capt.,	Cothren's Hist.,	785
Smith, Robert,	Cothren's Hist.,	785
Smith, Samuel,	Cothren's Hist.,	785
Smith, Stephen,	Cothren's Hist.,	785
Southworth, William,	Cothren's Hist.,	786
Sperry, Ambrose,	Cothren's Hist.,	785
Sperry, Eli,	Cothren's Hist.,	786
Sperry, Enoch,	Cothren's Hist.,	785
Squire, Abiathar,	Cothren's Hist.,	786
Squire, Gideon, Capt.,	Cothren's Hist.,	786
Squire, Joseph,	Cothren's Hist.,	786
Squire, Thomas, Jr.,	Cothren's Hist.,	786
Squire, Thomas 3d,	Cothren's Hist.,	786
Standclift, William,	Cothren's Hist.,	786
Starr, Elisha,	Cothren's Hist.,	786
Steele, Elisha, Sergt.,	Cothren's Hist.,	785
Steele, John, Sergt.,	Cothren's Hist.,	785
Steele, Luke,	Cothren's Hist.,	785
Stewart, William,	Cothren's Hist.,	786

Name	Authority	Page
Stevens, Aaron,	Cothren's Hist.,	786
Stevens, Daniel,	Cothren's Hist.,	786
Stiles, Joseph,	Cothren's Hist.,	785
Stoddard, Abijah,	Cothren's Hist.,	785
Stoddard, Adjutant,	Cothren's Hist.,	785
Stoddard, Amos,	Cothren's Hist.,	785
Stoddard, Anthony,	Cothren's Hist.,	785
Stoddard, Curtiss,	Cothren's Hist.,	785
Stoddard, Cyrenius,	Cothren's Hist.,	785
Stoddard, Eli,	Cothren's Hist.,	785
Stoddard, Ichabod,	Cothren's Hist.,	785
Stoddard, James, Capt.,	Cothren's Hist.,	785
Stoddard, Luther,	Cothren's Hist.,	785
Stoddard, Nathan, Capt.,	Cothren's Hist.,	785
Stoddard, Philo,	Cothren's Hist.,	785
Stoddard, Thomas,	Cothren's Hist.,	785
St. John, Adonijah,	Cothren's Hist.,	785
Stratton, Thomas,	Cothren's Hist.,	786
Strickland, Moses,	Cothren's Hist.,	786
Strong, Adino,	Cothren's Hist.,	785
Strong, Anthony,	Cothren's Hist.,	785
Strong, Benjamin,	Cothren's Hist.,	785
Strong, Benjamin, Jr.,	Cothren's Hist.,	785
Strong, Charles,	Cothren's Hist.,	785
Strong, Daniel, Teamster,	Cothren's Hist.,	785
Strong, John, Lieut.,	Cothren's Hist.,	785
Strong, Josiah,	Cothren's Hist.,	785
Strong, Samuel,	Cothren's Hist.,	785
Strong, Uriel,	Cothren's Hist.,	785
Sturgess, Aquila,	Cothren's Hist.,	786
Summers, Asahel,	Cothren's Hist.,	786
Tallman, Ebenezer,	Cothren's Hist.,	786
Tallman, Peter,	Cothren's Hist.,	786
Taylor, Josiah,	Cothren's Hist.,	786
Thomas, Charles,	Cothren's Hist.,	786
Thomas, Charles, Jr.,	Cothren's Hist.,	786
Thomas, David,	Cothren's Hist.,	786
Thomas, Ebenezer, Lieut.,	Cothren's Hist.,	786
Thomas, Enoch,	Cothren's Hist.,	786
Thomas, Isaac,	Cothren's Hist.,	786
Thomas, Jacob,	Cothren's Hist.,	786
Thomas, Jeremiah,	Cothren's Hist.,	786
Thomas, John,	Cothren's Hist.,	786
Thomas, S.,	Cothren's Hist.,	786
Thorp, David,	Cothren's Hist.,	786
Titus, Joel,	Cothren's Hist.,	786
Tomlinson, ———, Com.,	Cothren's Hist.,	786

Litchfield County Revolutionary Soldiers

Name	Authority	Page
Tomlinson, David,	Cothren's Hist.,	786
Tomlinson, David, Lieut.,	Cothren's Hist.,	786
Tomlinson, Henry,	Cothren's Hist.,	786
Tomlinson, Thomas,	Cothren's Hist.,	786
Tomlinson, Timothy,	Cothren's Hist.,	786
Tomlinson, William,	Cothren's Hist.,	786
Tona, Jethro,	Cothren's Hist.,	786
Tongue, Jonathan,	Cothren's Hist.,	786
Torrance, Ezra,	Cothren's Hist.,	786
Torrance, Joseph, Corp.,	Cothren's Hist.,	786
Torrance, Joseph,	Cothren's Hist.,	786
Torrance, Samuel, Jr.,	Cothren's Hist.,	786
Torrance, Samuel, Capt.,	Cothren's Hist.,	786
Torrance, Thomas,	Cothren's Hist.,	786
Torrance, William,	Cothren's Hist.,	786
Tossel, John,	Cothren's Hist.,	786
Touseley, Nathaniel,	Cothren's Hist.,	786
Trowbridge, Elihu, Lieut.,	Cothren's Hist.,	786
Trowbridge, Philemon,	Cothren's Hist.,	786
Tucker, Daniel,	Cothren's Hist.,	786
Turrill, John,	Cothren's Hist.,	786
Turrill, Samuel,	Cothren's Hist.,	786
Tuttle, Aaron,	Cothren's Hist.,	786
Tuttle, Andrew,	Cothren's Hist.,	786
Tuttle, Nathaniel, Capt.,	Cothren's Hist.,	786
Tuttle, Thomas,	Cothren's Hist.,	786
Twiss, Jonathan,	Cothren's Hist.,	786
Vandyke, Peter,	Cothren's Hist.,	786
Wagner, Daniel,	Cothren's Hist.,	786
Wagner, David,	Cothren's Hist.,	786
Wakeley, Abel,	Cothren's Hist.,	786
Wakeley, Abiel,	Cothren's Hist.,	786
Wakeley, Henry,	Cothren's Hist.,	786
Wallace, Thomas,	Cothren's Hist.,	787
Waller, Daniel,	Cothren's Hist.,	787
Waller, Thomas,	Cothren's Hist.,	787
Walker, Abel,	Cothren's Hist.,	787
Walker, David,	Cothren's Hist.,	787
Walker, Elisha,	Cothren's Hist.,	787
Walker, Isaiah,	Cothren's Hist.,	787
Walker, Joseph, Capt.,	Cothren's Hist.,	787
Walker, Joseph, Jr.,	Cothren's Hist.,	787
Walker, Josiah,	Cothren's Hist.,	787
Walker, Peter,	Cothren's Hist.,	787
Walker, Samuel,	Cothren's Hist.,	787
Walker, Simeon,	Cothren's Hist.,	787

Name	Authority	Page
Walker, Zechariah (alias Nathan)	Cothren's Hist.,	787
Warner, Daniel,	Cothren's Hist.,	786
Warner, Ebenezer, Lieut.,	Cothren's Hist.,	786
Warner, Eliphaz,	Cothren's Hist.,	786
Warner, Elizur, Capt.,	Cothren's Hist.,	786
Warner, John, Capt.,	Cothren's Hist.,	786
Warner, Samuel,	Cothren's Hist.,	786
Warner, Saul,	Cothren's Hist.,	786
Warner, Seth, Col.,	Cothren's Hist.,	786
Warner, Thomas,	Cothren's Hist.,	786
Ward, Macock,	Cothren's Hist.,	787
Ward, Samuel,	Cothren's Hist.,	787
Warden, Joseph,	Cothren's Hist.,	787
Washburn, Edmond,	Cothren's Hist.,	787
Washburn, Edward,	Cothren's Hist.,	787
Waters, Joseph,	Cothren's Hist.,	787
Watson, James, Hon.,	Cothren's Hist.,	787
Waugh, Buel,	Cothren's Hist.,	787
Way, Ira,	Cothren's Hist.,	787
Way, Isaac,	Cothren's Hist.,	787
Wayland, John,	Cothren's Hist.,	787
Weeks, John,	Cothren's Hist.,	787
Welch, Ithuel,	Cothren's Hist.,	787
Welch, Luke, Sergt.,	Cothren's Hist.,	787
Welch, Michael,	Cothren's Hist.,	787
Wells, Benjamin,	Cothren's Hist.,	787
Wells, David,	Cothren's Hist.,	787
Wells, John,	Cothren's Hist.,	787
Wentworth, G.,	Cothren's Hist.,	787
Wheaton, Jonathan,	Cothren's Hist.,	787
Wheaton, Roswell,	Cothren's Hist.,	787
Wheeler, Adam,	Cothren's Hist.,	787
Wheeler, Agur,	Cothren's Hist.,	787
Wheeler, Archelaus,	Cothren's Hist.,	787
Wheeler, Benjamin,	Cothren's Hist.,	787
Wheeler, Benjamin, Jr.,	Cothren's Hist.,	787
Wheeler, Elnathan,	Cothren's Hist.,	787
Wheeler, John, Capt.,	Cothren's Hist.,	786
Wheeler, Lemuel, Dr.,	Cothren's Hist.,	786
Wheeler, Seth, Capt.,	Cothren's Hist.,	786
Wheeler, Silas,	Cothren's Hist.,	787
Wheeler, William, Com.,	Cothren's Hist.,	787
Whipple, Joseph,	Cothren's Hist.,	787
White, Joseph,	Cothren's Hist.,	787
Whitney, John,	Cothren's Hist.,	787
Whittlesey, Asaph,	Cothren's Hist.,	787
Whittlesey, John,	Cothren's Hist.,	787

Name	Authority	Page
Whittlesey, David,	Cothren's Hist.,	787
Whittlesey, Martin,	Cothren's Hist.,	787
Wilcoxson, Ephriam,	Cothren's Hist.,	787
Wildman, Benjamin, Chap.,	Cothren's Hist.,	787
Wilkinson, Abraham,	Cothren's Hist.,	787
Wilson, Samuel,	Cothren's Hist.,	787
Wiscott, Joseph,	Cothren's Hist.,	787
Wood, James,	Cothren's Hist.,	787
Woodman, Samuel,	Cothren's Hist.,	787
Woodward, Noah,	Cothren's Hist.,	787
Woodward, Noah, Jr.,	Cothren's Hist.,	787
Wooster, Hinman,	Cothren's Hist.,	787
Wott, Adam,	Cothren's Hist.,	787
Wright, Charles, Jr.,	Cothren's Hist.,	787
Youngs, David,	Cothren's Hist.,	787

Supplementary List.

Castle, Abel,	D. A. R. Lin. Book Vol. XVII.,	164
Culver, Timothy, Sergt.,	D. A. R. Lin. Book Vol. XXVIII.,	276
*Curtis, Abel,	D. A. R. Lin. Book Vol. XXI.,	174
*Curtis, Elnathan,	D. A. R. Lin. Book Vol. XXI.,	174
Deming, Phineas,	D. A. R. Lin. Book Vol. V.,	201
Dudley, Asa,	D. A. R. Lin. Book Vol. XIII.,	150
Foot, Abraham,	D. A. R. Lin. Book Vol. XX.,	25
Gilbert, Isaiah,	D. A. R. Lin. Book Vol. XVII.,	190
Hooker, Ira,	D. A. R. Lin. Book Vol. XX.,	237
Hooker, James, Jr.,	D. A. R. Lin. Book Vol. XXIV.,	14
Hubbard, Thomas,	D. A. R. Lin. Book Vol. XIII.,	151
Hurd, Nathan, Capt.,	D. A. R. Lin. Book Vol. XXVII.,	88
Martin, Nathan,	D. A. R. Lin. Book Vol. XVII.,	197
Martin, Reuben,	D. A. R. Lin. Book Vol. XIX.,	226
Murray, Solomon,	D. A. R. Lin. Book Vol. XIV.,	236
Skeels, Truman,	D. A. R. Lin. Book Vol. XVI.,	145
Smith, Elihu,	D. A. R. Lin. Book Vol. XXV.,	208
Stillman, Joseph,	D. A. R. Lin. Book Vol. X.,	167
Warner, Benjamin,	D. A. R. Lin. Book Vol. XXII.,	208

Woodbury

These names appear in the list in Cothren's History of Woodbury and also on lists of other towns. Woodbury was a great recruiting station and many probably enlisted there who resided elsewhere.

Allen, Nathaniel,
Aspinwall, Caleb,
Balcomb, John,
Balcomb, Nathaniel,
Bates, Ephraim,
Beach, John,
Blakesley, Samuel,
Brown, James,
Butler, Abel,
Cash, Africa,
Castle, William,
Churchill, Oliver,
Davenport, John,
Dunbar, Joseph,
Field, Nathaniel,
Gould, John,
Holt, Nicholas,
Hudson, John,
Hunt, William,
Hungerford, James,
Jewett, Caleb,
Johnson, Amos,
Kellogg, Samuel,
King, David,
Mallory, David,
McIntire, Henry,
Mills, Samuel,
Munn, Justus,
Murray, Noah,
Northrop, Amos,
Phelps, Darius,
Porter, John,
Potter, Daniel,
Potter, Sheldon,
Rood, John,
Seymour, Moses, Capt.,
Smith, Abraham,
Sperry, Ambrose,
Stannard, Samuel,
Taylor, Joel,
Taylor, John,
Taylor, Simeon,
Thomas, Joseph,
Thompson, John,
Tuttle, Ichabod,
Wheeler, Nathan,
White, John,
Woodruff, John,
Woodruff, Hawkins,
Wright, David,
Wright, Freedom.

www.ingramcontent.com/pod-product-compliance
Lightning Source LLC
Chambersburg PA
CBHW051047160426
43193CB00010B/1097